Dedication

We dedicate this book to our brothers in Christ living in the U.S. including those who are not yet saved but who are destined to be our brother through faith in Christ. And to their children and families. May you discover a secure place to stand with the Lord and a new partnership with His Sovereignty as He deals with the earth in this ultimate time.

D0968119

THE ARC OF EMPIRES

Seeing God in the Crisis In America

Scott Webster

with Marlon Jameson

SWM Publishing
Marietta, GA

Unless otherwise indicated, all scriptural quotations are from the
New International Version (registered), NIV (registered), copyright ©
1973, 1978, 1984 by International Bible Society. Used by permission of
Zondervan Publishing House.

Scripture verses marked NKJV are taken from the New King James version of the Bible. Copyright © 1982 by Thomas Nelson, Inc. Used by permission. All rights reserved.

Scripture verses marked NET are taken from the New English
Translatioun of the Bible. NET Bible® copyright ©1996-2006 by Biblical
Studies Press, L.L.C. netbible.com All rights reserved.

The Arc of Empires
Published by:
SWM Publishing
1860 Sandy Plains Road, Suite 204-410
Marietta, GA 30066
ISBN 0-9818466-2-0

Copyright © 2013 by Scott Webster
All rights reserved.
Reproduction of text in whole or in part without the express written consent
by the author is not permitted and is unlawful according to the 1976 United
States Copyright Act.

Cover Design: Daniel Bodinof & Khyron Danclair
Book production by:
Silver Lining Creative, *A Division of Pivot Point Publishing*
SilverLiningCreative.com
PivotPointPublishing.com
Cover illustration is protected by the 1976 United States Copyright Act.

Printed in the United States of America.

Contents

Preface

This book provides a spiritual explanation for the crisis in America and the nations of the earth. It delves into political, economic and social issues, but at the core of the book is a word from God that brings light and illumination to what is taking place in our nation right now and what will happen in the future. God is dealing with the nations, and America finds itself at the center of Divine purpose. We must discover what He is doing and how He expects us to respond.

There are a number of people who we specifically had in mind in writing this book. First, this is for our brothers in Christ who have been walking faithfully and consistently with God. You have prayed, repented and worked, yet there is deep frustration because the nation continues to deteriorate. This word from God does something that is personally very important to us: it explains why the nation has continued to spiral downward despite the prayers and efforts of so many good people, while at the same time providing spiritual direction and a way forward. It is intended to reignite faith and hope in your spirit, to point you towards God and His goodness, and to remove any aspect of being unconvinced concerning God's purpose for you, your family and the nation.

This book is also for a second category of "brothers" — those who are our brothers but don't know it yet. It is for those who are destined to come into the Kingdom of God, but who remain trapped in the system of this world. You are not yet saved and perhaps there is an insufficient understanding of the nature of God. You may be thinking that He is judgmental and vindictive and that life in the future will be hard and bleak. This book is intended to bring hope and redefinition to the harvest of souls yet to come in to His glorious Kingdom.

What the Book is Not

Now that we have established what the book is and who it is for, it would also be helpful to describe what the book is not.

It is not political in the sense that it doesn't fit into the categories which seem to dominate the thinking about the nation. The first of these trumpets that America is plunging downward while enthusiastically enumerating all of its ills. But neither can this book be categorized into the second class which waves the flag and insists the nation will be restored to greatness tomorrow (or if not tomorrow, at least at the next election).

We can also say that it is not simplistic or religious. For many this will be unlike other books you have read because it doesn't provide a narrow or one dimensional answer. We can assure you it won't cover the same old ground and it won't push upon the nation tired answers that don't work. While not religious, we are unapologetic in our spiritual outlook and want to state plainly that it is based on principles from the Word of God which we apply to believers who have faith in Christ.

Finally this isn't a word of doom. It doesn't focus on things the nation has done wrong that have made God angry. There may be many of these things not only in our nation but in every nation of the earth–but that is not the angle of this book because that is not what God spoke to us. God is redemptive. This is a core part of His nature and therefore all words from God must come from a heart filled with redemptive hope and possibilities.

Our Premise – There Must be an Explanation

The times are tumultuous and uncertain, but God does have a purpose. As we think about what is happening there are three possible explanations for all the crises:

Possibility #1: These events are random, each one occurring without any connection to the others or to any central purpose. This view holds that things will return to normal soon enough. To believe this we have to accept that the economic meltdown, political impasse, wider social decay, natural disasters of epic proportion – all of which are occurring with increasing frequency and intensity – are purely arbitrary and therefore ultimately meaningless. This possibility holds the view that God either does not exist, or, if He does, He is not actively involved in the affairs of men and nations.

Possibility #2: A second explanation is that the devil has gone crazy and is taking the earth to hell in a hand basket. He has unleashed crisis, or at the very least mankind has degenerated to some low state and all hell is breaking loose, and we have to pray that God gets involved to "fix it." At the core of this view is that the nation is decaying, and there is a cry of alarm and a search for solutions that are usually political in nature. This view is held widely among believers, but there is a problem with this scenario in that it contradicts the definition of God as the Sovereign One, in charge of all things including light and darkness, blessing and disaster. The problem is this: if we say that God is not in charge, then we must answer the question of "how can He be God when all these things are happening outside of His will?"

The first possibility denies God exists and puts man at the center (because man defines what is important and meaningful rather than God), while the second explanation accepts that there is a God but denies His sovereignty and wrongly places darkness front and center. Therefore both of them must be rejected.

Possibility #3: The third and final explanation is that God is completely in charge, He has a purpose and He is leading the earth towards ultimate outcomes. The crises are not random and darkness, though it does exist, is not in charge. God is firmly in control and despite people's misconceptions, He is working in the earth through the crises. This explanation refutes the thin, plastic view of God which offers simple and quick answers which evaporate before our eyes when the next crisis hits. Realizing that God is in charge even in the darkness and tumult of the earth, produces internal confidence and strength, releasing within us boldness and the power of a relevant faith. It redefines our view of God Himself and as a result we are given the opportunity to become more like Him. Therefore it is not only an explanation for the crises, it is also a call to personal transformation. It is the view we put forth in this book which contains these two key aspects: a) a spiritual explanation for the crisis, b) a call to personal transformation as we embrace Biblical definitions for how we must live in the crisis as we move towards the End of Time.

Who we Are and What is our Agenda

It's difficult to define yourself in a paragraph or two, but a few high points might help you know a little bit about us. I (Scott) had a pretty ordinary childhood as our family moved from one military base to another as my father flew for the Strategic Air Command (SAC) division of the Air Force. During an uneventful college experience I got saved in 1980 and immediately began to grow and be groomed by the Lord as a leader in the church particularly in the area of the prophetic. There are some formative things in my background and some key processes that shaped me; for those who want to know more you can access the link below.[1]

It was in my role as a budding prophetic leader that I met Dr. Noel Woodroffe, who invited me to Trinidad in

---

[1] www.arcofempires.com/authors

1990 as part of a larger team for a national prophetic conference, an event that proved pivotal for both him and me. A strong relational connection emerged with Noel and I returned to Trinidad every year to minister both in his church (Elijah Center) and the apostolic network he subsequently founded. Going to Trinidad was not just another ministry trip for me. Beyond the ministry there was a "discovery" of God's relational design and I found refuge and divine placement in connection with him and within the apostolic network. I have been serving with and standing alongside Dr. Woodroffe ever since.

It was in 1995 on one of my visits to Elijah Center that I met Marlon Jameson, who had recently come to the church and was himself being targeted by God as an emerging leader. The Caribbean is located in what is referred to as America's "backyard" so Marlon grew up very conversant with the happenings and norms in the U.S. If my academic career was uneventful Marlon's was intense, including graduate degrees in international relations and experience lecturing in the International Relations field.

We are distinct individuals with varied educational, cultural and personal backgrounds. Marlon and Alana's children are the same age as mine and Kathy's grandchildren. But we have come to be very much alike in the most important ways: our value system and our worldview have been radically changed and defined by the Kingdom of God in a way that diminishes the definitions imposed on us by our distinct cultures.

Beyond being co-authors Marlon and I serve on the leadership team of Congress WBN. We will explain our name more fully later in this volume, but we can say here that the name "Congress" is not related to a government entity. It describes our global apostolic network of churches, along with other initiatives into the fields of education, commerce, leadership, community building, etc. This book is an initiative of Congress WBN designed to resource the Body of Christ including those who will yet come to faith in the last great harvest. This book is the third in a sequence entitled The New Prophetic Dimension Series; a set of writings that describe the current positions of the prophetic designed to resource the Body of Christ.

It is written to equip you to know what God is doing in the earth and to prepare the Body of Christ for greater partnership with the Lord and His End-Time purposes. It is not the will of God for any of us to be fainting in terror or in distress and He does not want us clinging to irrelevant definitions that cannot be sustained in light of the onset of crisis. As God's people, we have a right to know what God is doing. We must make sense out of the chaos of our world and defeat the perplexity of the times.

A brief editorial note before we begin. I am the lead author of Parts 1 and 2, which contains a prophetic scan of America's history and assessment of where the nation stands right now, as well as what will happen in the future. Marlon is the primary author of Part 3, which contains a series of teachings and spiritual realities that empower us to stand securely in a time of crisis. Although there were clearly demarcated responsibilities, the entire book is a collaborative work to the point that each page is the product of our combined efforts, individual section assignments notwithstanding.

It is our prayer that just as we came to a place of joint ownership of the word from God that forms the basis of this book, that it would now become your spiritual possession also. We are asking for God to fill you with insight and faith to stand strongly while crisis rages all around us.

Part 1

DESCRIBING THE LANDSCAPE

Whatever exists now has already been, and whatever will be has already been; for God will seek to do again what has occurred in the past.

Ecclesiastes 3:15 (NET)

Chapter 1
"Modern America is Like Ancient Egypt"

I was enjoying a week at the beach with my family when the Lord spoke this word into my heart and mind. It is a short phrase, only six words, but the impact of it is vast and its ramifications so far reaching that it requires this book to explain and apply. I didn't "see" or "hear" the six words. Instead the concept appeared in my mind as a fully formed and solid chunk of divine thought. As a revelation from God it was new and inspired, yet it wasn't totally out of the blue. Several things were at work within me that formed a context into which the word fell and found a place of resonance.

I was already writing and I intended to continue while on vacation, sneaking in a few minutes early or late as the days unfolded. I was working on a book that addressed the widespread chaos that seems to have been unleashed on America and the rest of the world – Marlon was assisting me with that project also. From the financial meltdown to natural disasters to wider society which seems compelled to plunge deeper and deeper into darkness, it is clear that something is going on and we were seeking to explain what is happening and why.

My week at the beach was in mid-2012 during the run-up to the presidential election, one of the most divisive times in American political history. I was especially grieved by the way believers were thinking about the choice between presidential candidates, and in a wider context, how the church has approached politics generally over the last 20 years. People didn't seem to have a spiritual context through which to see what is happening in America and the preoccupation with political solutions (or alternately political problems that must be fixed) robbed people of the ability to see the spiritual reality behind all of the tumultuous events. I was trying to finish that book before the elections to help bring understanding, but I was not succeeding in my self-imposed time frame.

There was another key factor that defined the context this word from the Lord fell into. The week before our beach trip I was part of an intense week-long seminar where our leaders, about 200 people from 30+ nations who form the upper management structures of our Congress, had gathered for a critical meeting that changed the direction of our corporate advance. Over the past few years God had been leading us towards greater engagement with the Body of Christ. God loves His Church and the more we grew and matured the more we found Him burdening us to love the Body of Christ also. Not just love them as in holding a view of benevolence towards those who are redeemed, but love demonstrated by sacrificially serving and looking for ways to more deeply engage with God's people.

Loving the Body of Christ included freely providing them whatever resource He had given to us and offering ourselves as a place of sanctuary for those who will flee from those portions of the Church which are corrupt or vastly undernourished. I am speaking specifically of the Church in America, which has been used so powerfully by God but which now finds itself, at least in some segments, unequipped to withstand the crises which are hitting with increasing intensity.

As I sat on the beach and watched families playing or went to dinner with my family, these are the things that were going through my mind. I was offended at the thought of someone else's children suffering because they are living in a place of intense crisis and confusion when there is spiritual resource that could easily be given. The Lord had activated a sense of compassion within me and the care and burden for my brothers simply would not turn off, and it was during this time that God opened to me this sweeping prophetic insight:

Modern America is like Ancient Egypt

It is from this word that we derived the title of the book. It describes the Arc of Empires, one ancient and one modern, which compare so perfectly that one is a prophetic metaphor for the other.

A Word from God is Empowering

The word from God surprised me–not because it is bad, but because I asked Him about America, and He pointed me towards understanding Ancient Egypt. I wouldn't have imagined in a million years that an ancient empire holds the key to understanding modern America but the comparison leapt into my heart and mind.

> *This prophetic word is like that scanner – it looks beyond the surface of things.*

It was almost like a scanner you go through at the airport with the new wave millimeter technology, where you put your hands above your head and the thing scans your physical image to ensure passengers are not carrying anything dangerous. That's what the voice of God was like in this case. God hit the start button, the scanner started on one side and moved all the way around, revealing a clear image of what is really happening in the nation. This prophetic word is like that scanner — it looks beyond the surface of things and brings revelation in three powerful dimensions:

a) It empowers us to have discernment of the spiritual reality that lies behind the political, economic and social happenings in America today. What is happening with the government, the economy, in wider society? We can't afford to have mere opinions. In the midst of so many chaotic and destabilizing events we have to know what is going on from God's point of view. The origin of the problems does not begin with politics or economics. It begins with God. He is doing something and there is a coherent spiritual explanation that makes sense of all the crises and turmoil, and He wants us to know what He's doing. This prophetic comparison lifts us above the crises and lets us see into God's mind, which is the only thing that can remove confusion and change us from being destabilized to being secure.

b) It reveals the future as we look to see what will occur in America in the years to come. The prophetic has the power to prepare us for what will come. This comparison is powerful because the history of Ancient Egypt becomes predictive for us. It reveals the pattern of impending events, where things are going and what kind of events will occur in America in 2014 and beyond. Prophetic understanding shapes our outlook and prepares us for imminent happenings which are ready to be released into the earth. These things *will* come and God wants us to be equipped to live in a future He is speaking about now.

c) It more fully unveils the nature of God as the Sovereign One. Perhaps the greatest need for believers today is to come to new sight of the Sovereignty of God. The Church has known Him as the one who blesses, saves, delivers and provides for us — and of course He does do all those things. But beyond knowing God in the immediacy of our personal lives, we have not fully comprehended His bigness and His intention and ability to use all things for His purpose. This is especially true for those of us living in the U.S., a nation used so powerfully by God in history but which is now in decline. There are so many bad things happening: economic meltdown, natural disasters, political instability, societal decay, etc., that it looks to our natural minds that God is not in charge. This prophetic comparison helps us understand that just as God was totally in control of and directing the outcomes in Ancient Egypt, so He is directing life in Modern America. It brings us into clearer sight of God as the One who is superintending the sweep of history in the United States, both the centuries of blessing and also now during a time of destabilization. This prophetic comparison reveals that we don't need to pray for God to get involved in the crisis. He is already involved and His purpose is redemptive.

Our Approach

We have organized the book into three parts. In this first section entitled Part 1 we introduce the word from God that is the core of this book. We then define the terms we are using to ensure we are all on the same page, and look at how God speaks through metaphors since the word from the Lord was given as a metaphor. We explain what we are comparing between the two empires and why.

Part 2 details the prophetic comparison that Modern America is like Ancient Egypt through examining twelve (12) *Key Prophetic Similarities* which are categorized into four phases that track the development within both empires: a) *The Ascent* b) *The Decline* c) *The Hardening* and d) *The Confrontation*. As we go through them you will see how perfectly the two empires compare; it's almost as if God put the account of Ancient Egypt in the Bible for us to understand as we approach the last days.

The third section will focus on how God expects us to respond to what He is doing. It explains specific initiatives the Spirit is birthing within us to make us ready for ultimate events, a series of characteristics we call *Transformation Imperatives*. These can be applied by every believer and within every church—these imperatives have the power to equip us to walk in partnership with God in a day of crisis, and therefore to lift us "above" the crisis.

God is calling us to Himself and lifting us into greater partnership as we move towards the End of Time!

Chapter 2
Defining our Terms

As soon as we refer to Egypt, many think of the Arab Spring that erupted across the Middle East in 2011 and which continues to make headlines. Protestors gathered in Cairo's Tahrir Square to seek a change of government policy, ousting Hosni Mubarak and, in the first democratic election in Egypt's history, elected Mohammed Morsi. Morsi had strong support from the Muslim Brotherhood, a political, religious and social force in Egypt and throughout the Islamic world. However, after a year in power Morsi was removed and the military cracked down on his supporters in a bloody episode that saw more than 600 killed in one day. While the political instability in the region will continue for some time, recent events in Egypt and the Middle East are *not* what God meant when He spoke to us about *Ancient* Egypt.

We have to define our terms; otherwise some might impose meanings or a view of world events to this prophetic word that God did not intend. We begin, therefore, by identifying what the terms mean which are contained in the word itself. The word of the Lord is that *Modern America is like Ancient Egypt* — one is a metaphor for the other. So what is "Ancient Egypt" and what is "Modern America?"

a) Modern America

The United States is a distinct nation that has physical borders and an economy that can be measured. On the most basic level America is that nation we can see before us – fifty states with 300+ million people, etc. But America is much more than that. More than any other nation it shaped the 20th century through its military strength, the power of its political ideals and the vast reach of its economy. The broad global influence of the nation can be seen in the following facts cited in 2004:[2]

✔ More than half of the 500 largest global companies are American, five times as many as second ranked Japan. Sixty-two of the top 100 brands are American.

✔ Educationally America is still top flight, at least at the university level. Eight of the top 10 business schools are American, and of the 1.6 million students enrolled in universities outside their own countries, 28 percent are in America (compared to 14 percent in second ranked Britain). More than 86,000 foreign scholars were in residence in American educational institutions in 2002. The nation ranks first in Nobel prizes for physics, chemistry and economics.

✔ The United States attracts nearly six times the inflow of foreign immigrants as second-ranked Germany.

All of these indicate America has played a formative role on the world stage. Its greatest influence however, is economic. It is the present globalized economy that we are including in our definition of "Modern America". Each of the 190+ nations have their own unique history and culture, not to mention a measurable economy of their own and some of

> *More than any other nation, America shaped the 20th century through its military strength, the power of its political ideals and the vast reach of its economy.*

[2] Statistics taken from *Soft Power*; the Means to Success in *World Politics*, Joseph S. Nye, Jr., (NY, 2004)

those nations are now growing faster and are in better health than the U.S. economy. So why equate the global economy with America?

America's economic model won in a global competition against all other economic ideologies. It outperformed Communism, Socialism and every other kind of economic theory put forth in various nations. The Soviet Union went bankrupt and imploded, ultimately dissolving after going through a period of political and economic reform. The process of reform began in the late 1980s and eventually the economy was completely revamped and made Capitalistic (more like America's).

But the best example is China. They dismantled their centrally planned economy and modified their policies to include private ownership and market-driven trade. The Chinese economy took off like a rocket and is now the second largest economy in the world. It is projected to overtake the U.S. as the world's largest somewhere around 2016.

> *The word God gave us describes God's dealings with the entire earth, not just one nation.*

When China liberalized their economic policy, Deng Ziaoping minimized the importance of economic ideology with a Chinese homily: *"It doesn't matter if a cat is black or white, so long as it catches mice."* America built the economy that catches mice.

But an economic system does not exist in isolation – it has a context and nations had to adopt certain value systems that go along with American economic norms. Things like private ownership of property, market-driven pricing via supply and demand and a strong profit motivation. Other values also undergird the system: self-will, competition, greed, debt spending, consumerism, etc. American capitalism, undergirded by political freedom and economic opportunity, created an environment for responsible people to work hard and create wealth, but it also provided a context for people to express intense levels of self-indulgence and place personal agendas in front of everything else.

When we say Modern America then, we are referring to this vast global economic system and the values that drive it. The quest for profit and personal gain has overtaken the entire earth and which serves as the core driver of all nations and which describes Biblical Babylon (Is 14, Rev 18). All the nations, despite the cultural and historic uniqueness of each, have bought into a global system out of necessity – they must keep their economy going and to do that they are required to be part of the globalized economy. The driving force in the nations is economic and it is this that is making the world "one" as they come together around one common quest.

To illustrate this further let's compare two very different demographic groups. The first is Wall Street executives, many of them American males in their 50s and 60s. The second, young Chinese women in their 20s embarking on

> *The economies of the nations are so tied together via economic necessity and internet connectivity so as to form one global system.*

careers and having to make decisions about marriage and family.[3] A saying among the young upwardly mobile female in China is "*I would rather cry in a BMW than smile on a bus,*" indicating that not having a family would hurt, but they prefer the car and wealth over the economic restrictions imposed by a family. They don't want a husband if it means not being supported in the lifestyle they prefer. No different than the Wall Street executives who invented new ways to make higher profits, practices that were at the core of the global financial meltdown. These executives were motivated

---

[3] The fact that there are many exceptions on Wall Street, including female executives as well as people of other national backgrounds, underscores the premise.

by the large year-end bonuses that allow them to buy a second house in the Hamptons, take vacations to Europe, etc. The two groups speak different languages, grew up in vastly different societies, are from different generations, yet they have the same core drivers that define their lives. As the End draws nearer and Babylon matures and approaches ultimate judgment, the greed of man is intensifying and self interest is being pursued more ruthlessly.

Ironically, recent events in Egypt fit within this category of Modern America because when you scratch beneath the surface of things and look beyond the warring factions, the underlying issues are people who want greater political freedoms and more economic opportunities. They are fighting with the power structures, both political and religious, that want to keep people locked down. In 2011 pictures and videos from Tahrir Square raced across the internet to inform the entire world of the strong arm measures used by the police, and authorities in the nation actually shut down the Internet in an attempt to limit international outrage. But the move backfired, limiting the thousands of banking and business transactions that speed across Egypt's "internet economy" so essential to every nation.

Whether it is Westerners on Wall Street, those in the Middle East agitating for different governments, people in the emerging economies in Brazil and South Africa or a new class of Chinese professionals, all are grappling with the same core issues. Babylon is calcifying and hardening and being more clearly manifest as the dominant spiritual culture in all the nations of the earth. And the economies of the nations are so tied together via economic necessity and internet connectivity so as to form one global system. Therefore this prophetic book is relevant for people from across the nations because Modern America is a globalized reality. God is dealing with the entire earth not just one nation.

b) Ancient Egypt

It would be more accurate to think of Ancient Egypt as Biblical Egypt, where historic events involving Pharaoh, Joseph and Moses are recorded in the books of Genesis and Exodus. It could also be thought of as Pharaohnic Egypt.

The first thing it represents is a national entity or an empire that was dealt with by God. Joseph, and later Moses, interacted with political leaders and the social systems of the empire, bringing the will of God to bear in the nation. Through this ancient empire we can see how God used prophets to interact with the nation and His purpose in Ancient Egypt provides keen insights into His purposes in America today. So Ancient Egypt represents a nation used by God for His purpose and which became a global empire as a result.

As a nation Ancient Egypt also provides a window into how a national entity varies in its interaction with God's people. It is here that we first see the Israelites being formed into a nation, growing and prospering within the borders of Ancient Egypt and given favor by God. But over time the political tide turned and the people of God who once were favored and blessed in the nation began to be marginalized and eventually enslaved. Ancient Egypt represents a political change of fortune as a nation varies in its stance towards God's people.

Ancient Egypt also provides insight into the thing that lies behind a nation — the unseen spiritual forces that influence political, social and economic life. It was this unseen dimension that brought massive economic growth in the form of seven years of abundant harvests and then seven years of famine. The same spiritual reality had a dramatic effect on immigration policy. Entire nations came down to Egypt, and some lived there long after the famine was over. So behind economic cycles, immigration policy and demographic changes in a nation lies an unseen spiritual force — Ancient Egypt represents that.

In addition Ancient Egypt represents the power of darkness in its ultimate form: death or mortality. Mortality is not just a description of the process by which people grow old and die. It is the last enemy and it fights against all attempts to break its hold over us (1 Co 15:26). Ancient Egypt represents death, which resists God's authority and is hardened against the Lord's commands. God hardened Pharaoh's heart and it set up a titanic con-

> *Ancient Egypt represents people being liberated from the clutches of mortality itself.*

frontation between God and His enemies. Ancient Egypt represents resistance, darkness and oppression in the spirit realm. It is a place of confrontation and crisis. And ultimately, Ancient Egypt represents people being liberated from the clutches of mortality itself.

There is One More Group...

There is a third distinctive group embedded within the metaphor the Lord has given us — the Israelites who were slaves in the empire that God was crashing. God dealt with His people distinctly and separately because His purpose for them differed vastly from His purpose for the empire. He was assaulting the empire, but He was resourcing His people. The Israelites lived and worked within Ancient Egypt, but their trajectory was in opposition to what was happening in wider society. While society was splintering and breaking down, the people of God were becoming more cohesive. In Ancient Egypt family life got so bad that the firstborn in every house was killed but in the nation of God every child was not only safe, they were also spiritually aware — they were dressed and ready for exit on the night that God moved.

Our ancient brothers demonstrate that it is possible to live in the midst of crisis but be full of faith and strength. Moses and the people of Israel walked through the crises and were brought out with a mighty hand (Ex 32:11). The Israelites were transformed from a weak and broken society under a cruel taskmaster to an identity-filled people who knew their God. Moses stood before Pharaoh and demanded liberation, and when the powers of Ancient Egypt refused to let them go they participated with God in releasing plagues that wrecked the society. It was the people of God who were behind the crises.

> *Our ancient brothers demonstrate that it is possible to live in the midst of crisis but be full of faith and strength.*

The comparison with Ancient Egypt abounds with powerful insight, clear spiritual patterns and unambiguous instructions for how we must live as the Body of Christ in the earth. We must prosper and grow in faith while living within an empire that God is assaulting and dismantling for His redemptive purpose.

Chapter 3
Ancient Egypt as Prophetic Metaphor

We use metaphors in everyday life without even realizing it. I am writing this on my laptop using "windows," and people often refer to the eyes as "windows of the soul." Neither computers nor pupils are literal windows — the word is a metaphor to describe something else. Or consider that the financial crisis in 2008 is referred to as a "meltdown" even though there were no high temperatures and a nuclear reactor wasn't involved. A metaphor is a literary device – which means it is a way of saying or writing something. It produces understanding by saying one thing is like another thing that it is normally unrelated to.

Metaphors are one of the primary ways the prophets conveyed God's mind to His people. For example, God instructed Hosea the prophet to marry a harlot and he compared her to His people who broke covenant and were like an unfaithful wife to Him (Ho 9:1). In another example, as Israel prepared to invade the land of Canaan, Moses reminded them that in a previous encounter the Amorites chased them *like a swarm of bees*, but now they could be assured that God was going ahead of them *like a devouring fire* to drive out their enemies before them (Deut 1:44, 9:3). *An unfaithful wife, a swarm of bees, a devouring fire* — each is part of the rich metaphoric language of the Bible.

15

Jesus Used Metaphors

Jesus used metaphors extensively; when he saw crowds who were aimless he had compassion on them and described them as being *"like sheep without a shepherd"* (Mt 9:36). People are not literally sheep, but the need for protection and leadership is brought to life by comparing us to weak and defenseless animals. He continued with the sheep metaphor when He told His disciples they were being sent out *"like sheep among wolves."* They were innocent and pure and their mission thrust them into a spiritually hostile environment. Therefore they should be *"wise as serpents but harmless as doves"* (Mt 10:16). *Sheep, shepherds, wolves, serpents and doves...*Jesus looked at nature and said "it is like that."

At one point Jesus said openly that he was looking for a way to describe those who refused to hear John the Baptist: *"To what can I compare this generation?"* he asked, indicating he had thought about it and searched for an apt comparison. Having found a perfect parallel, He then said *"They are like children sitting in the marketplaces and calling out to others: we played the flute for you and you didn't dance; we sang a dirge and you didn't mourn"* (Mt 11:16-17). Of course they weren't actually children nor did they play a flute or sing. But when Jesus used metaphoric language everyone understood these religious leaders were like spoiled, immature children. The metaphor also implied they could have used a good spanking!

A Prophetic Metaphor with a Biblical Basis

The comparison God has given to us is Biblically based because Ancient Egypt is described in detail in the Word of God. Embedded within the metaphor is a vast store of Biblical history, which is unchanging and eternal and which provides Biblical safeguards that guide us into

> *The prophetic metaphor provides Biblical safeguards that guide us into full and correct interpretation.*

full and correct interpretation. That is especially important in a time when "prophetic words" and dreams seem to be pulled out of the ether. Some lead people off the beaten trail into dangerous and unbiblical territory.

Let us restate our premise: we are *not* saying that Modern America *is* Ancient Egypt. The word from God is that Modern America is *like* Ancient Egypt; we are comparing the two empires. Historically America has been compared with Biblical Israel so it may seem strange at first to be comparing it with Ancient Egypt. But consider that Biblical Israel as a nation was a small tribal monarchy with little influence beyond the Middle East. They won wars against more powerful neighbors because God helped them. Ancient Egypt and Modern America, on the other hand, had a military/industrial complex that allowed them to dominate other nations. It was the powerful Egyptian military that God drowned in the Red Sea, refuting their ability to impose their will by force.

The two empires share other geopolitical similarities that were not present in Biblical Israel. For example, both empires enslaved a specific ethnic group upon which they built their economic dominance. This sets them apart from Biblical Israel, whose economic system was built on equity, justice and distribution based on instructions from God, while Ancient Egypt's was built on exploitation, extraction and hoarding (they built store cities to stockpile their wealth, Ex 1:11). Beyond these obvious geopolitical similarities that could apply to many historic empires, there are four important points of comparison which reveals that God dealt with each empire in a very similar way.

a) The ***Divine Purpose*** for each empire is remarkably similar. There is always a point to God's actions. He does not do things randomly and looking at Ancient Egypt helps decode God's purpose in Modern America. This metaphor explains why God made the nation great.

b) The ***Processes*** by which God dealt with each empire are very comparable. He sent believers into the nation to establish it and to bring spiritual counsel and wisdom in how they should be built. He breathed upon the economy and made it expansive. And he confronted the nation with crisis and destabilization.

c) The ***Sequence*** of God's dealings with both nations follows the same timetable or progression. The progression of God's dealings is seen in the four phases of the Ascent, the Decline, the Hardening and the Confrontation.

d) The ***Maturity Emphasis*** for the people of God was the same in Ancient Egypt as in today's global Church. A primary emphasis in both eras was God transforming His people into a powerful nation in their own right. This prophetic comparison proclaims that while there is crisis in the nations there is great spiritual resource being released to God's people. It is a time of transformation, increasing faith in the Sovereignty of God and hope!

Metaphors are powerful, and they are Biblical. This prophetic word about America was given in the form of a metaphor to allow us to understand God's complex movement in the nation. God is speaking because He wants us to know how to interact with the events taking place now, as well as what will come in the future.

Part 2

A PROPHETIC COMPARISON

Chapter 4
He Makes Nations Great

An arc describes movement and dynamic progression that takes place over time as nations go through phases of growth and development. A single verse describes the full Arc of Empires. Job needed only about a dozen words to effectively explain the Sovereignty of God within the rise and fall of nations. It was during the Ascent that God was making this nation great.

> *He makes nations great, and destroys them; he enlarges nations, and disperses them.*
>
> *Job 12:23*

The phrase "God makes nations great" indicates that behind the natural events of America's growth God was at work. God makes nations great. He is involved with their expansion and their development. God *makes* and He also *enlarges*. Both words are verbs that indicate God is actively involved in a two part process. First He works over time in the building up of a nation and once it is strong, the nation expands and is stretched out like a blanket — that is the literal meaning of the word for "enlarge." The words *make* and *enlarge* describe a budding empire that grows in strength and then has the capacity to exert its influence beyond its national borders.

This two part process describes America's ascent very accurately. The U.S. went from being a few colonies settled by early Europeans who landed in Jamestown and other places along the Eastern seaboard, and the first centuries produced primarily agricultural prosperity empowered by political stability and one federal union which shared currency, law, language and

> *God enlarged the U.S. so that American norms were spread over the earth, covering the nations like a blanket.*

culture. The word "ascent" means to rise and since it came into being, America's growth was demographically, geographically and economically expansive primarily in the agricultural era of the 18th and 19th centuries.

America then exploded during the Industrial Revolution and became the dominant nation of the 20th century. God enlarged the nation's influence so that American norms were spread over the earth like a blanket. Whether it is the economic system built in the U.S., its political model adopted by many in the last century, its powerful military stationed all across the earth or even its culture adopted by many outside its borders, America's influence was enlarged far beyond its shores. God made America great and He enlarged it in a process that started at the early founding and continued until in the 20th century the nation sat like a colossus over the economic, political and military realms in the nations.

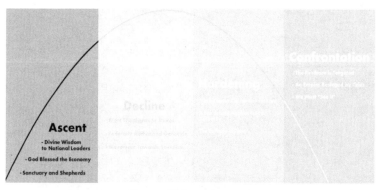

Graphic: Arc 1

The Ascent is seen in the upward swing of the Arc, pictured in this graphic along with the following three Key Prophetic Similarities that examine how God worked to build and enlarge the empire of Modern America

> *Key Prophetic Similarity 1:*
> Divine Wisdom to National Leaders

> *Key Prophetic Similarity 2:*
> God Blessed the Economy

> *Key Prophetic Similarity 3:*
> Sanctuary and Shepherds

Chapter 5
Key Prophetic Similarity #1:
Divine Wisdom to National Leaders

Have you ever seen a movie or a graphic that shows an apartment building where the outside wall is suddenly removed? In one apartment the guy is sitting and watching TV, in another kid's are playing, in a third someone is busy in the kitchen, etc. That is what the Scriptures about Ancient Egypt provide — a stripping away of the façade of a nation which allows us to see God's involvement with great clarity.

The account in Genesis includes a description of how God directly impacted: a) the economic cycles of Egypt b) the ascent of an empire to a place of regional dominance among the nations c) immigration patterns of nations crossing borders and settling in foreign lands d) the devastating effects of enslaving an entire demographic group. The Biblical narrative strips away the facade behind the political, economic and social realms to show us plainly that God was behind the developments of Ancient Egypt as a "heathen empire." And

> *The Founding Fathers were aware they were interacting with a spiritual realm filled with values and power not of this earth.*

although it manifested as economic growth and later as decline, God was behind these events, orchestrating and moving nations around for His purpose.

How Did God Do It?

God blessed Ancient Egypt and interacted with them in many ways. He gave the king a dream and then he sent Joseph to interpret it (Gen 41:14-15). The Bible defines Joseph as a prophet and he was given prophetic insight into the meaning of Pharaoh's dreams. Pharaoh understood he was dealing with a spiritual dimension when he talked with Joseph. He was aware that Joseph was a representative of a spiritual realm filled with values and a power not of this earth. Egypt's ascent was not an accident of history, nor was America's. God was behind the growth and development of both empires and there was a conscious awareness of God's providential hand upon the nation.

The Bible describes Joseph's role in Egypt as one who would *"teach their senators wisdom"* (Ps 105:22) and Joseph himself understood that God had made him *"a father to Pharaoh"* (Gen 45:8). There was divine instruction and heavenly involvement which was at the core of Egypt's ascendance as a nation. God gave them wisdom, He showed them how to build and His Spirit worked with Egypt to make them dominant in the nations. He blessed their economy and tutored them how to manage such a vast, global enterprise. So God was overtly involved in the founding and building up of America. He gave the founding fathers wisdom and favor. Many of the founding fathers and architects of the nation were believers. Others were not, but they still understood that God was involved in the birthing and building up of the nation.

How did input from God impact America? A study was done to determine the source of the Founding Father's successful ideas, including examining more than 15,000 documents and 3,000+ direct quotes. Each quote and document was traced back to its original source to find the origin of the ideas put forth by the architects of the American nation and more than one third came directly from the Bible. One author who refers to this study indicates that Biblical concepts were utilized in the formation of American government, citing specific verses:[4]

✔ The three branches of federal government taken from a description of God's nature *"For the LORD is our judge, the LORD is our lawgiver, the LORD is our king; it is he who will save us"* (Is 33:22)

✔ The rationale for separation of powers based on human nature and tendency towards corruption *"The heart is deceitful above all things and beyond cure. Who can understand it?"* (Jer 17:9)

✔ The basis of tax exempt status for churches and ministries *"You are also to know that you have no authority to impose taxes, tribute or duty on any of the priests, Levites, singers, gatekeepers, temple servants or other workers at this house of God"* (Ezra 7:24)

God blessed America and the founding fathers knew it. James Monroe declared in a statement to Congress *"When we view the blessings with which our country has been favored...our attention is irresistibly drawn to the source from whence they flow. Let us then, unite in offering our most grateful acknowledgments for these blessings to the Divine Author of All Good."* Pharaoh, in response to Joseph's prophetic insight which prospered Egypt's economy, declared *"Can we find anyone like this man, one in whom is the spirit of God?"* (Gen 41:37-38).

> *America's founders recognized that God had granted them wisdom, blessing and favor and positioned America in a unique place among the nations.*

The president and the emperor could have been reading from the same script. America's founders recognized that God had granted them wisdom, blessing and favor and posi-

---

[4] David Barton, *America's Godly Heritage*, (1993, TX), p 24 & 25

tioned America in a unique place among the nations. Pharaoh knew it. The founding fathers knew it. And we have to know it and acknowledge it if we are going to come to a place of true prophetic insight.

Chapter 6
Key Prophetic Similarity #2:
God Blessed the Economy

I think it was in a macro-economics class that they hammered the principle of supply and demand. It's pretty simple. The price of a good is determined by a point at which two factors intersect: a) the quantity supplied b) the quantity demanded. Where those two meet determines the price of the good. For example, you can buy fill dirt for about $15 per ton here in Atlanta. It's in abundant supply and the demand is low in that you can get it anywhere — it's all around us. Gold on the other hand is $1734 per ounce on the day I'm writing this. You have to check it every day because it varies...based on supply and demand.

In Ancient Egypt God arranged the ultimate "supply and demand" scenario using food, something in great demand. God provided massive harvests, building up their supply and then He provided information about a future famine that would cause acute demand. The Lord prepared them to become the wealthiest of nations. An intense famine that lasted for seven years, combined with the foreknowledge to store up grain, forced nations to buy grain from Egypt, swelling their national treasury and their global influence. This Key Prophetic Similarity declares that God prospered the national economy for His purpose.

Economic System that Produced Blessing

Egypt was blessed by God and raised up as an economic power, drawing many nations in need of its resource. All the nations depended on Egypt for financial supply and it controlled a large percentage of global GDP. Joseph radically changed the economic environment of Egypt,

> *If Egypt's system could be summarized as "managing harvests and feeding the nations," then America's would be "freeing the markets and creating wealth."*

buying up property for the nation during the famine and instituting a massive national economy whereby every farmer continued to give twenty percent of their proceeds to the king, a practice which lasted long after he died (Gen 47:26). Divine favor was on Egypt, not only giving them seven years of abundance, but tutoring them on how to steward the increase in order to build the nation into an economic powerhouse that dominated the earth. So it was also in America.

Free enterprise released a spirit of innovation and risk taking that produced huge growth which continued over a period of centuries. But it was more than that. It was the direct blessing of God upon America's economy that caused the nation to prosper and one of the key factors was the practice of Capitalism. If Egypt's system could be summarized as "managing harvests and feeding the nations," then America's would be "freeing the markets and creating wealth." Both Egypt's harvests and America's markets experienced the hand of God upon them for expansion.

Purpose of the Blessing: Connect the Nations

Egypt's prosperity had a purpose: to connect the nations through trade and economic necessity. God accomplished that through famine: *"When the famine had spread over the whole country, Joseph opened the storehouses and sold grain to the Egyptians, for the famine was severe throughout Egypt.* **And all the countries came to Egypt** *to buy grain from Joseph, because the famine was severe in*

> God empowered America to become the leading economy in the earth, and then used its strength to create a global system of trade.

all the world" (Gen 41:56,57). "All the countries came to Egypt" to take advantage of their resource. The famine was severe "in all the world." God effectively orchestrated a global economic system through the famine that made the nation tremendously prosperous. Egypt's wealth had a purpose beyond the blessing – to connect the nations.

The massive wealth of America served the same purpose. God empowered America to become the leading economy in the earth and then used its strength to create a global system of trade. The nation used its abundance to rebuild defeated empires in Germany and Japan following WWII. Those three nations (America, Germany and Japan) were the three largest in the global economy for many years. The nation then used its influence to formalize a global order of trade through the construction of the Breton Woods institutions (IMF, the World Bank and GATT/WTO). This allowed the U.S. to become the central arbiter of global finance and trade policy.

The nations of the earth could never come together around any other issue. Politically they had diverse systems which were incompatible. Some systems were closed and autocratic while others had open, democratic political systems. The culture and history of each nation are unique and served to divide them as nations fought one another or held historical enmity. The only thing all nations have in common is the desire for economic growth. And to participate in the global economy every nation must make its economy compatible with American norms. China is still a Communist nation yet it has engaged in vast commerce with the nations of the earth, especially America which buys a large percentage of its manufactured goods.

It's called globalization. Everyone wants a piece of the pie. The United States served as a pivot point for economic life, leading to ever increasing growth and greater and greater interdependence among the nations. In Ancient Egypt God used famine and abundance to connect nations. In our day He has used trade agreements, banking and financial institutions and increased markets for goods. Just as nations streamed into Ancient Egypt to buy food in order to survive, economic oneness is a necessity in the modern world.

Chapter 7
Key Prophetic Similarity #3
Sanctuary and Shepherds

God has always protected and preserved His people. Even in times of intense persecution the Church has grown and had thriving spiritual life. And wherever they have been located, the people of God have supplied a preserving dimension to human life, or what the Bible calls salt and light because the virtues that come from God and are resident in us guide and preserve society (Mt 5:13,14). We are calling these two realities sanctuary and shepherds.

Both Ancient Egypt and Modern America provided sanctuary for God's people. Joseph said that God sent him to Egypt for *"the saving of many lives"* (Gen 50:20). His family would have starved if he had not been sent to prepare a place of refuge for them. Jacob told his sons on repeated occasions to go to Egypt and buy grain *"so that we may live and not die"* (Gen 42:2, 43:1). When Joseph finally revealed himself to his brothers he said, *"Do not be distressed and do not be angry with*

> God sent believers to America to preserve them, and they provided a strong basis for faith in the nation.

yourselves for selling me here, because it was to save lives that God sent me ahead of you" (Gen 45:5). Egypt became a sanctuary for God's covenant people who fled the famine in their homeland.

This parallel is so clear it almost explains itself, especially when we look at the history of the original immigrants who came to America. Among the first were the Puritans, so called because they sought to live a holy life and as a group their mission was to reform (or purify) the church in England. The established church largely rejected their efforts to reform it, making it a criminal offense to attend Puritan worship services and putting a price on the head of the more influential leaders. The Puritans finally fled to America and John Winthrop wrote of his decision to emigrate *"All other Churches of Europe are brought to desolation...and who knows but that God hath provided this place to be a refuge for many He means to save out of the general calamity."*[5] It sounds as if Joseph in Egypt and Winthrop in America experienced the same reality. Each was used by God to create a refuge for His people. God sent believers to America to preserve them, and they provided a strong basis for faith in the nation.

Shepherds in Ancient Egypt

Believers in Ancient Egypt were shepherds, that was their occupation and Joseph told his brothers specifically to identify themselves as such when Pharaoh asked them (Gen 46:33). Egyptians didn't like shepherds, they found them repulsive (Gen 46:34). They weren't concerned about pastoral issues. Ancient Egypt was focused on building an empire. They cared about a sustainable economy, political issues and the building of store cities. The Bible makes it clear that this was two different classes of people with different priorities.

What is the spiritual significance of this distinction? When God sent Joseph's family into Egypt — a family of shepherds — He was strategically inserting a spiritual com-

---

[5] Quoted in *The Light and the Glory*, Peter Marshall and David Manuel, Expanded and Revised Edition, (MI, 2009), p 195

ponent into secular society. Throughout the Bible we see that shepherds represent several important spiritual realities: a) they provide guidance and protection to people (sheep), caring for their souls and their spiritual lives b) they guide community life as a shepherd does a flock of sheep, keeping society together and moving cohesively c) they protect against wolves, or elements that seek to ravage humans and destroy their families d) they bring emphasis to the importance and sanctity of every human life — it is the shepherd who leaves the ninety-nine to find the one stray sheep.

The shepherding aspect provided by believers in Modern America softened society, taking the hard edges off the empire. If a nation focuses only on the political and economic aspects of life, society becomes too brutal and harsh. The addition of a shepherding component brings care and value to people beyond simply what they are able to produce. The shepherding reality was so vital and intertwined within Egypt that even Pharaoh told Joseph to find the best shepherds to tend his flocks. A shepherding and spiritual dimension was welcomed on the federal level and it impacted political realities (Gen 47:6). The same occurred in America, where presidents counseled with and received prayer from men of God and church leaders — some because they genuinely valued it and others because they knew the strong Christian culture expected it.

> *The shepherding aspect provided by God's people softened society, taking the hard edges off the empire.*

There is another important aspect that defines Israel's role within Ancient Egypt — they were assigned to live in Goshen, a sub-region within Egypt. The word Goshen means "to draw near." It is a word describing proximity and relationship. When we combine the two key elements of the Israelites within Ancient Egypt, we see it was their spiritual values, their standards and their relationship with God that brought a care for individual human life (shepherding) and the nearness of God (Goshen) to Ancient Egypt.

Shepherds in Modern America

Likewise the people of God within the U.S. exercised a strong shepherding function within the empire on many different levels. They shepherded or stewarded moves of God that were birthed within the church in the U.S., giving themselves to spiritual growth and development and tracking the emphasis of the Holy Spirit within each move. Believers also built churches to

> *Believers were inserted into the empire to emphasize spiritual values, to shepherd wider society, and to bring the nearness of God to the nation.*

bring people into the truths God was emphasizing, and under-shepherds cared for the flock God had given to their charge, bringing personal moral values and a strong family emphasis to society (1 Pet 5:1-4).

Christian schools provided strong shepherding — protection, nurturing and resource — to generations of children. Both the Christian school phenomenon and the home school movement originated in the U.S. — for a long time other nations had nothing to compare it to, though now it has caught on in places outside of the U.S. also. In one sense the Church in America became an instrument of shepherding for the wider Church that existed in the nations by exporting the truths and spiritual realities God had given to them. The wealth of the American economy combined with the generosity of believers fueled the missionary thrust which allowed believers living in America to buy plane tickets, print books, send missionaries, etc.

In America the Church was esteemed and received for hundreds of years, serving as a redemptive force that God had embedded deeply within the fabric of the nation. Believers in America were like the children of Israel in

Ancient Egypt, inserted into the empire to emphasize spiritual values and to shepherd wider society and bring the nearness of God to the nation. Christianity in America brought the values and principles of heaven and the presence of God very near to American society, providing guidance to an empire that grew into a powerful global force.

But at some point that changed. Over a process of time those whose function had been to bring the nearness of God to the nation through their shepherding capacity were marginalized and their values were largely rejected. As a result the American empire has become more secular, more brutal and more hostile to the Spirit of God. And America was plunged into a time of decline.

Chapter 8
He Disperses Them

He makes nations great, and destroys them; he enlarges nations, and disperses them.
                                                    Job 12:23

America was made great by God and for centuries enjoyed His blessing upon its economy and institutions. But the nation is now in decline and that is also of the Lord because God also *destroys* and *disperses* nations. The Hebrew word for "disperse" in Job 12:23 is *nachah*; it means to guide, to govern and to lead. In the NASB it is translated *"He enlarges the nations, then leads them away."* The key thought here is that God is the one who guides the nation into captivity and breaks their strength by splintering them or leading them away from the ability to build cohesively. God's leadership and redemptive purpose are being exerted both in the ascent and the decline.

> God's leadership and redemptive purpose is being exerted both in the ascent and the decline.

We can't look at the times and seasons of America or any nation apart from considering the nature of God, who *"Has made everything beautiful in its time"* (Eccl 3:11). In the well known chapter of Ecclesiastes 3, Solomon listed 28 particulars, some positive (a time to build, a time to laugh, a time to heal), others negative (a time to tear down, a time to weep, a time to uproot). We tend to see only the positive things as good and beautiful: a time to be born, a time to laugh and a time to dance, etc. But the Scripture is all inclusive – God makes *everything* beautiful in its time; even downturn, dispersal and hardening are used for His glorious purpose. Because it is God who manages the dissolving of a nation's strength, we can be assured there is redemptive intent behind the full arc of movement.

Redemption only makes sense if we look at life through the eyes of God. If we live within the capacity of our human minds, then life is a series of blessings and setbacks, triumphs and tragedies. Nations rise and fall — they are made great and then broken. But if we live in the mind of God it is one seamless plan of redemption that is unfolding and bringing mankind back to Him. From God's point of view dispersal and destruction are just as "good" as blessing and being made great. The Word of God is true despite our emotional responses to loss or difficulty — God says it is good and made beautiful by Him.

You can also see the graphic indicates Decline beginning well before the empire reached its highest point. Once the upward growth and ability to exert dominance begin to fade, the nation is in a state of decline, even when it remained the dominant nation of the earth. American decline is not recent. We have set the time of Decline as beginning sometime around 1976 based on some key events of the era which all mark deterioration: a) 1976 was the first year America had a negative trade balance (it imported more than it exported) and the trade deficit has grown every year since b) Vietnam was the first war America lost, drawing to an end at the fall of Saigon in 1975 c) in the mid to late 1960s the proliferation of drugs and "free love" (immorality) was foisted by the devil upon American young people, undercutting the social fabric of the nation and beginning to re-define and deconstruct the family d) The Supreme Court ruled to legalize abortion in the 1973 decision of Roe v Wade. e) the Watergate scandal in the early 1970s undercut confidence in the American political process and eroded confidence in authority in general, weakening the family and government at the same time.

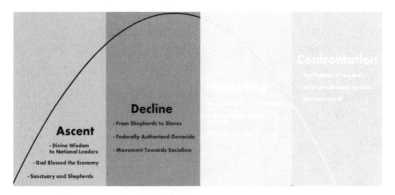

Graphic: Arc 2

We will examine the Decline through three Key Prophetic Similarities:

> ➤ *Key Prophetic Similarity 4:*
> From Shepherds to Slaves

> ➤ *Key Prophetic Similarity 5:*
> Federally Authorized Genocide

> ➤ *Key Prophetic Similarity 6:*
> Movement Towards Socialism

Notice also that the direction of the text in the graphic is going upward in the Decline phase even though the Arc is showing the opposite. Even though the nation is in Decline, the purposes of God are moving forward. The graphic is portraying two distinct entities: the empire, which is beginning to decline, and God's global and eternal purpose, which is always ascending and moving forward. The Decline has negative impact in the nation, but the overall result is a furtherance and advancement of the purposes of God.

Chapter 9
Key Prophetic Similarity #4
From Shepherds to Slaves

It is clear in America that attitudes toward believers have changed, and not for the better. The influence of Christianity in America is decreasing drastically to the point that to be a believer who holds firmly to Biblical principles is considered to be both ignorant as well as intolerant. The same thing occurred in Ancient Egypt in the attitudes towards the people of God. In the beginning, Joseph was put in charge of the entire nation and prophetic insight led the society. People of faith had favor in the halls of government, and part of the blessing of God upon Egypt was the way they received Joseph and his family. But over time that place of favor was lost. The Bible says *"Then a new king, who did not know about Joseph, came to power in Egypt"* (Ex 1:8).

The new Pharaoh didn't esteem the spiritual reality that was a major part of the empire's beginnings. He rejected Joseph and he rejected Joseph's God. Conversations occurred in the corridors of power, and decisions were made to marginalize and enslave the believers: *"They put slave masters over them to oppress them with forced labor, and they built Pithom and Rameses as store cities for Pharaoh"* (Ex 1:11). For a time, the nation's objectives and practices were in close sync with the values of the people of God, but that changed and a clear distinction was drawn between the

43

two separate entities: a) the nation of Ancient Egypt, with its own interests and agenda b) the people of God.

Marginalized and Enslaved

Despite the massive blessing of God on the nation and the contributions of believers to public life, the influence of Christianity in America has been minimized and people of faith marginalized within

> *The influence of Christianity in America has been minimized and people of faith marginalized within the nation.*

the nation. American society and culture have largely abandoned the original values, authentic morality and spiritual realities that were the basis of people's individual faith — values that served the nation so well. To put it more bluntly, society has vomited us out.

The nation is moving strongly towards definitions that completely contradict Christian ethics and norms. Not only are same sex marriages being legalized, but those who disagree are defined to be judgmental. We are not allowed to stand on a moral principle while declaring our love and care for all humans. Our refusal to compromise on this point is defined by others to be homophobic, judgmental and hateful — a recent sign at a pro gay rally declared *"hate is not a family value."* So not only is society seeking to eliminate moral principles that are eternal, they are also aggressively seeking to remove any alternative viewpoint. It is not a single politician who has turned the tide in America and it is not recent..

The Church in America has also become enslaved. Our bondage is not a natural prison or back breaking physical labor. We are enslaved by the shackles of materialism and bowed down under the heavy yoke of carnal success that shrivels the spirit-man and makes us internally weak. It is a bondage that robs us of true prophetic insight. The Church in America today struggles to hear God just as our brothers who were enslaved in Ancient Egypt: *"So Moses spoke thus* to the children of Israel; but they did not heed Moses, because of anguish of spirit and cruel bondage" (Ex 6:9). God told Moses that he had heard the people's cries but when Moses was sent with a new spiritual initiative to liberate the people, they couldn't hear it because slavery had broken their spirit and shriveled their faith in God.

What Are We to Do?

It may be helpful to clarify what we are *not* saying here. We don't believe that there aren't **any** believers working to influence public policy or that all political leaders are against the Church and anti-faith. Clearly that is not true. We personally know people who labor for God in the public arena, as well as officials who are genuine believers. Yet even with the efforts of good people, the wider system has become more hostile towards God. The parallel with Ancient Egypt makes it clear that while this is distressing to us as believers and harmful to the nation, it is also part of God's redemptive plan.

Because of the increase of wickedness, the love of most will grow cold,

but he who stands firm to the end will be saved.

Matthew 24:12,13

There is increasing wickedness in the earth and we must ensure it does not destroy our faith. We are living in an environment of increasing toxicity and it will get worse. Darkness is intensifying and Jesus warned that in that environment of the End Times we must stand firm and endure and not allow our love for God and for the brothers to grow cold. What is growing cold? It is putting our hope in political solutions while our confidence and faith in God's purpose wanes. It is becoming discouraged because the prevailing trend of society is towards more and more wickedness.

It is compromising our faith because the wider environment doesn't receive us with joy.

Darkness may have marginalized our influence upon society, but nothing must ever corrupt our hearts, shrivel our faith or cause our love to grow cold. We are filled with hope because our faith is not in political solutions. Our hope is in the Lord. God is using the hostility and the change of fortunes to purify His Church in the nation and to deliver us of the false hope that the nation itself has the answers.

Chapter 10
Key Prophetic Similarity #5
Federally Authorized Genocide

Few things reflect the decline of the nation as starkly as the practice of abortion, allowed in America since the 1973 ruling of the Supreme Court in Roe v Wade. Pharaoh — the holder of federal power in Ancient Egypt — also made the killing of children legal in Ancient Egypt: *"So Pharaoh commanded all his people, saying," Every son who is born you shall cast into the river, and every daughter you shall save alive"* (Ex 1:22). At the core of the modern abortion debate is the question of when life begins. Consider these medical facts that chronicle the unborn child's development:[6]

a) At the moment of conception forty-six genes are combined, twenty-three each from the mother and the father. At that initial point of formation the embryo has a distinct genetic identity that is different from the mother, a biologically unique identity it will have for life b) At two weeks there is a discernible heartbeat and the heart is circulating blood that is not its mother's but blood it has produced c) At forty-three days the unborn child has detectable brain waves, and by nine weeks the fetus has developed a unique set of fingerprints d) By the end of the twelfth week all the organs are functional and the baby can cry. All of these developments occur in the first trimester of the unborn

---

[6] Quoted in *Abortion: A Rational Look at an Emotional Issue*, by R.C. Sproul, (FL, 1990), p 50

child's life, a distinct human that has not only unique physical characteristics, but also a spiritual and moral destiny.

Beyond the medical facts we have the Word of God. David expressed gratitude to God when he prayed *"For you created my inmost being; you knit me together in my mother's womb. I praise you because I am fearfully and wonderfully made; your works are wonderful, I know that full well. My frame was not hidden from you when I was made in the secret place. When I was woven together in the depths of the earth, your eyes saw my unformed body. All the days ordained for me were written in your book before one of them came to be"* (Ps 139:13-16).

These verses reveal that the biological growth of a fetus in the womb is a process superintended by God, who "created me" and "knit me together in my mother's womb." The baby was "woven together in the depths of the earth." The words used to describe the process that occurred during gestation are revealing. Man was "created" or formed by God. The word used describes a craftsman skillful in forming things. The word for "woven together" literally means to sew together different colors as a weaver or embroider of cloth. The reference here is to the various and complicated tissues of the human frame — the tendons, nerves, veins, arteries and muscles "as if" they had been woven and intricately joined to form one human body.

The formation of a fetus in the womb is not just a physical process of gestation. It also is the creation of a spiritual being with a moral and spiritual identity. When David sinned with Bathsheba and killed her husband Uriah, his repentance included a reference to being formed in sin in his mother's womb *"Surely I was sinful at birth, sinful from the time my mother conceived me"* (Ps 51:5). There is a "me" at conception, a unique identity that has a specified moral state. In Psalm 139:16 God saw the unformed body — the word is *golem* and it's the Hebrew word for embryo — the only place it occurs in the Bible. The word literally means to be folded, with the idea that the process of development in the womb is the physical development and unfolding of a created life.

(An important note must be inserted here for those who have aborted a child. The facts and positions listed in this chapter are not for the purpose of condemnation but to define the key spiritual and moral realities which are at the core of the issue. For those who have aborted a child there is forgiveness through repentance and a healing of the guilt and shame. Moses murdered an Egyptian and Paul brutally tortured and killed many believers, yet they were each forgiven, redeemed and raised up as perhaps the greatest spiritual leaders of their respective eras.)

Sovereignty Triumphs

God is Sovereign. He is over light *and* darkness and even when evil is being propagated God is able to accomplish His purposes in the midst of the carnage. Moses was put in a basket and in an act of faith his mother placed the basket in the reeds of the Nile, where he was soon rescued by Pharaoh's daughter. God arranged for Moses to slip

> *God is over light and darkness, and even when evil is being propagated is able to accomplish His purposes in the midst of the carnage.*

through Pharaoh's murderous order and put the child right in Pharaoh's house as he grew into manhood.

Beyond Moses being preserved by God there is the spiritual drama played out upon his return to Egypt. Moses' name means "drawn out of the water" and the first plague released by the prophet was to turn the same Nile where babies were drowned into a river of blood (Ex 1:22, 7:20). The final plague is an even more dramatic act of Divine retribution. Moses' obedience to God released the ultimate plague that killed Pharaoh's firstborn son.

Some readers may disagree with the straightforward approach we have taken in this chapter. Others may think we haven't gone far enough since we haven't specifically advocated for a political solution such as an overturning of the legalization of abortion. Whatever one's view of the modern abortion debate, this prophetic comparison provides another clear parallel between how the sanctity of human life was diminished both in Ancient Egypt and Modern America.

Chapter 11
Key Prophetic Similarity #6
Movement Towards Socialism

One of the big concerns of many Americans is the increased government involvement in private life. Beyond "ObamaCare" and the wider government bail-out following the meltdown, there is a real concern that America's free enterprise system is being slowly eroded, dismantled and replaced by Socialism. In a poll of likely voters in the 2012 US election, 55 percent thought that "Socialist" was an accurate way of describing President Obama.[7] There is a functional merging of the governmental and economic realms to form one coherent governance system within Modern America, a reality also present in Ancient Egypt.

However we read the Biblical narrative in Genesis, the word which best describes the economics in Ancient Egypt is Socialism. Pharaoh imposed an additional 20 percent federal tax on all farmers and in addition to a drastic increase in taxes during the emperor's administration we also see a) a new federal department being created and more persons going on the government payroll b) increased government intervention into private business c) a state directed food distribution program, etc. Under Pharaoh the federal government took over the agriculture sector. Government grew, not shrank in Ancient Egypt.

---

[7] www.nationalreview.com/campaign-spot/230874/55-percent-likely-voters-find-socialist-accurate-label-obama, retrieved November 15, 2011

But because we have perspective we don't even think about Socialism when considering Joseph and Egypt's economy – we think about God's purpose. God wanted Joseph's family to migrate to Egypt so He caused a famine, but only after He orchestrated a government takeover of the agricultural sector during massive harvests. God had a purpose for the "movement towards socialism" in Ancient Egypt, and He has a purpose for America (and all nations) bailing out their economies in our day.

What is God's Purpose Now?

When the kings of the earth who committed adultery with her and shared her luxury see the smoke of her burning, they will weep and mourn over her.

Terrified at her torment, they will stand far off and cry: "'Woe! Woe, O great city, O Babylon, city of power! In one hour your doom has come!'

"The merchants of the earth will weep and mourn over her because no one buys their cargoes any more

Revelation 18:9-11

The 18th chapter of Revelation provides insight. It is a description of what happens at the end of time when an angel shouts from heaven and crashes the global economy. When that happens there are two groups of people who cry out in alarm — kings and merchants. In modern terms these are politicians and business leaders. Of the two, business leaders are noted as the world's *"great men."* In a Biblical comparison they rank first, above political leaders (Rev 18:23). The word "great" is the Greek word *megistanes*, which means a person of great importance and high status. The obvious meaning is that life at the End of time is driven by economics above all else. The economy is the chief thing and the pursuit of money defines life above all other priorities.

What is really happening is less of an ideological shift and more pragmatic. Nations are involved in economic survival and what has been called "Socialism" is the new economic order both for America and also for the other major economic blocs in the earth such as China, the EU, Russia, etc. The result is a utilitarian economic system that is neither purely Capitalistic nor Socialistic. It combines the worst of both worlds: the inefficiency of government planning combined with the intense greed which exists at the core of Capitalism. Thus the nations are moving closer towards the End Game — a combustible economic system that is both intensely greedy *and* grossly inefficient and ready for ultimate judgment. Governments are coming to a place of deep unification around sustaining an economic system that is precarious and vulnerable to shocks to the point that when an angel shouts from heaven it will collapse.

How Are We to Respond?

How are we as believers living in America supposed to respond to the "movement towards Socialism?"

"Rejoice over her, you heavens! Rejoice, you people of God! Rejoice, apostles and prophets! For God has judged her with the judgment she imposed on you."

Revelation 18:20

In a time of economic judgment there are believers thriving in the earth and the church is filled with apostles and prophets who lead and equip the people to live strongly in a time of crisis. We are commanded to rejoice when Babylon (the global economy) is judged by God and begins to fall. It is not distressing news because everything God does is good. Therefore it is important for us to see God's purposes being enacted beyond the decisions of politicians or the trajectory of the economy, and the command to rejoice clearly implies faith and confidence in God's Sovereignty. The people living at the end of time are not shallow believers or nationalistic in their focus. They know the Sovereign God who is dealing with the systems and all nations. We must see that the presence of economic chaos in the earth is an indication of the Sovereignty of God.

Chapter 12
He Deprives Leaders of Reason

We now move into the phase of the arc entitled the *Hardening* and the words in Job can be expanded beyond verse 23 since the following verses also apply:

He makes nations great, and destroys them; he enlarges nations, and disperses them.

He deprives the leaders of the earth of their reason; he sends them wandering through a trackless waste.

They grope in darkness with no light; he makes them stagger like drunkards.

Job 12:23-25

Once again we see the direct involvement of God in the destruction of empires: *He deprives* leaders of reason, *He sends* them wandering, *He makes* them stagger. In addition to showing us that God is actively engaged in the downturn, these verses also reveal a clear process of deterioration within an empire. It describes the way in which God deals with a nation when His purpose requires it to be broken.

The first thing God does is to deprive the leaders of their reason. The word used for "reason" has a two-fold meaning: the first describes the heart and soul of man, his conscience and his moral character that form the basis of decision making. The second meaning of "reason" is a person's knowledge, their competence and their ability to think through problems and resolve them. When we combine these two meanings, we understand that depriving leaders of reason involves two components: a) removing the moral compass and conscience which causes leaders to make ethical decisions b) weakening their ability to work through problems and implement solutions.

The next thing listed in the breaking process is God sending the nation wandering through a trackless waste. The words paint a picture of going around in circles and making no decisive progress

> *The earth is in crisis and desperately needs answers, but the leaders in the nations have been deprived of their reason.*

because there are no road signs — it is "trackless." Forward movement and strategic development are not possible in this environment because God has removed the roadmap. The place they are wandering is also described as a "wasteland." There is a clear implication of God drying up the financial resources of what was economically abundant in former times.

As a result of this the leaders of the earth *"grope in darkness with no light; he makes them stagger like drunkards"* (v 25). What unfolds is a doubly intense reality: the earth is in crisis and desperately needs answers but the leaders in the nations have been deprived of their reason. To grope in the darkness is to have no solutions and no understanding of what the real issues are. To stagger like a drunkard is to lack the ability to navigate and move forward. The issue is not a lack of activity. Leaders are groping and searching but not finding anything. They are staggering and stumbling but their movement is not purposeful and it doesn't take them where they want to go. The description by Job is an accurate portrayal of the state of the leaders of the earth today, who fit the combined meanings of the words we have highlighted. They have:

a) Lost their conscience and moral character

b) Have lost their competence and ability to think

correctly and are left searching for answers to the increasing complexity caused by decline

c) Look for signposts about what to do but find no indicators that direct them

d) No longer have the ability to budget and craft a strategic economic plan for the nation

e) Grope in the darkness and have an inability to see what the real issues are

f) Stagger like a drunkard with a lack of control

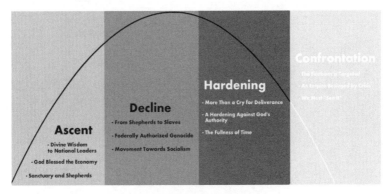

Graphic: Arc 3

As we move into the section on the *Hardening,* God's purpose becomes clearer. We can see how He uses both the powerful prayers of His people, crying out for deliverance and also an increasing hardening of the Darkness in the earth. Both accomplish His purpose. Once again the graphic includes text that is ascending in the category of the Hardening, symbolizing that although things are devolving and become darker, God's purposes are advancing and escalating just as they were in Ancient Egypt. The hardening of Pharaoh's heart was an upward progression of God's purpose, which required the empire to become fixed in its hostility to the Lord. The Hardening is captured by three Key Prophetic Similarities:

➤ *Key Prophetic Similarity 7:*
More Than a Cry for Deliverance

➤ *Key Prophetic Similarity 8:*
A Hardening Against God's Authority

➤ *Key Prophetic Similarity 9:*
Deliverance Comes in the Fullness of Time

Chapter 13
Key Prophetic Similarity #7
More Than a Cry for Deliverance

It was prayer in Ancient Egypt that caused God to initiate a new movement in the Earth. The people of God groaned and prayed and God heard the prayers of His people, which caused Him to remember His covenant and to confront Egypt.

> *Now it happened in the process of time that the king of Egypt died. Then the children of Israel groaned because of the bondage, and they cried out; and **their cry came up to God because of the bondage.***
>
> *So God heard their groaning, and **God remembered His covenant** with Abraham, with Isaac, and with Jacob.*
>
> *And God looked upon the children of Israel, and God acknowledged them.*
>
> Exodus 2:23-25 (NKJV)

Israel was enslaved for four hundred years. The Bible describes their experience as "cruel bondage" and it caused them to pray and groan. The word groan is the Hebrew *anach* and it means to sigh, groan or mourn. The groaning and prayers of our ancient brothers reminded God of His covenant made with Abraham, Isaac and Jacob: *Then He said to Abram: "Know certainly that your descendants will be strangers in a land that is not theirs, and will serve them, and they will afflict them four hundred years. And also the nation whom they serve I will judge; afterward they shall come out with great possessions."* (Gen 15:13,14). They were praying for political deliverance, but God's response was to remember His ancient covenant to bring them into their Promised Land.

God's covenant with Abraham represented a non-negotiable Divine objective, a promise so powerful that it subordinates everything else to its fulfillment. What God spoke to Abraham was going to be fulfilled and nothing could stop it. It was like a juggernaut steam-rolling through time towards the point of fulfillment. It was destined to crash on the shores of Egypt like a spiritual tsunami. His plan never included giving them a better life in Egypt or returning the nation to an earlier era when they enjoyed favor in the nation. They wanted political deliverance and they wanted the hard conditions under which they labored to end. But God had something much bigger in mind and what He heard was *more* than a cry for deliverance.

The Groaning of the Modern Church

It is no accident that one of the primary identifiers of the modern Church is prayer. Intercession, warfare prayer, worship and prayer…every kind of prayer has been going up before the Lord from the Church across the Earth. A number of churches and ministries have determined to make prayer a primary focus, meeting in shifts so that prayer goes up before the Lord 24 hours a day. Others gather believers in strategic meetings to pray and ask God for deliverance, while still others travel to key locations and make specific requests and appeals to heaven. It is impossible to catalogue the millions of prayers, and beyond that the internal groanings which have gone up to the Lord, but many fall into these broad categories:

a) People have been praying and repenting on behalf of an entire nation, often standing on Scriptures such as 2 Chron 7:14: *"If my people, who are called by my name, will humble themselves and pray and seek my face and turn from their wicked ways, then will I hear from heaven and will forgive their sin and will heal their land."*

b) There have been strong prayers for revival to sweep across the nation, and for the Body of Christ to come to a place of passion and commitment to the Lord.

c) Prayers (and efforts) towards greater unity in the Body of Christ have gone up as people sense the call of God to become more united and "one" before the Lord. Pastors and leaders especially have gathered to pray together and to lift one voice to God from their city or region.

> *God has something much bigger and more ultimate in mind than restoring America.*

d) Prayer to reverse the tide of Darkness in wider society, and for particular initiatives to be halted (abortion, gay marriage, etc.) and for other initiatives to be launched or reactivated (restoring prayer in schools for example).

What Has God Heard?

We have prayed fervently, yet despite our many prayers of repentance on behalf of the nation and our cry to God to restore America, things have gotten worse. Instead of restoring the nation in response to our groaning, God has launched a series of attacks which are shattering society. Our ancient brothers did not receive a "new and improved" Egypt and we will not experience a restored America. We must move from a passion for renewal of American society, because that is not our ultimate destiny. It is thinking too small, too nationalistic, too bound by pride in the history of the nation.

There is something far more important — God is giving us the power to journey towards His ultimate purpose. Like the children of Israel who were in bondage, God is preparing to deliver us from the bondage of mortality. He is empowering us with the required mentalities to move towards exit because He has heard as the Church prayed and groaned. Like our ancient brothers, we prayed one thing but God heard the real, underlying cry of our heart — it is *more* than a cry for deliverance.

God is now acting to bring to pass ultimate events. There is a clear sequence revealed in Exodus: prayers, confrontation, hardening and crisis leading to exit. In the process there were multiple interactions between Moses and Pharaoh, a drama that saw Pharaoh harden himself against the word of the Lord again and again.

Chapter 14
Key Prophetic Similarity #8
A Hardening Against God's Authority

It doesn't make sense that the more we pray the more the nation becomes hardened against God's purpose, but that is exactly what's happening. The hardening is against God's authority in the spirit realm, but it manifests in the nation in natural ways also. The word "hardening" in the original Hebrew carries two interesting meanings (Ex 8:15). The first is to be heavy with honor, abundance and glory. The second is to become dull, insensible and unresponsive. Combining the two meanings, "hardening" describes a condition where as a result of the accumulation of honor, abundance, influence and power someone, or in this instance an empire, starts to become increasingly dull, unresponsive and incapable of course correction. It is the classic effect of pride and arrogance.

Ancient Egypt's empire status, glorious history and meteoric rise along with Pharaoh's sense of his own power combined to fill the system with a sense of pride which made it incapable of hearing God. Instead it hurtled unstoppably towards an epic confrontation with God. It had become filled with its own sense of invincibility and greatness. It didn't need to heed anyone else and relied instead on its own proven wisdom and self-sufficiency. It inadvertently became blind and deaf to everything except its own imperatives and therefore sealed its own demise.

This is the path of all empires. There always comes a time when it has won too many times to even consider the possibility of defeat. It has overcome too many challenges to consider the possibility of failure. It has defeated too many forces of opposition to consider that the one it now faces cannot be overcome. It has weathered too many crises to think that it cannot come through the current one. This condition stems from a corruption within the human heart that lies at the leadership center of all empires in decline.

In Modern America, this condition expresses itself most clearly in leadership opinion about the current crises. Everyone is saying it is going to get better. They declare we have been here before, and like former times, we will rise again. There are repeated assurances that the massive and sprawling US economy will recover. No one is considering that the crisis we are experiencing is unprecedented. None say that the solution to the crisis lies outside of the lessons learned from past experience and accumulated wisdom. As a result, our options are being narrowed and the nation is heading even further into an inevitable downward spiral.

He Hardens Whom He Wants to Harden

For the Scripture says to Pharaoh: "I raised you up for this very purpose, that I might display my power in you and that my name might be proclaimed in all the earth."

Therefore God has mercy on whom he wants to have mercy, and he hardens whom he wants to harden.

Romans 9:17,18

There are three important dynamics that are revealed in God hardening Pharaoh, dynamics that are at work both in Modern America and the wider nations and systems of the Earth.

a) The increase in wickedness and opposition is a result of God's Sovereignty. God is over darkness and light, prosperity and disaster (Is 45:7). He utilizes all these things for His purpose. The hardness is not a triumph of evil. It is part of God fulfilling His purpose as He Sovereignly deals with the Earth. The phrase "I raised you up for this very purpose" indicates that the hardening is ultimately of the Lord. It may manifest in a political agenda, but it cannot be redressed in that forum because it didn't originate there. Nor can it be reversed by believers because it is an initiative of the Lord who declares "I raised you up" — God takes responsibility for the Hardening and no amount of prayer will change it.

b) God is glorified through the Hardening. Romans notes that through the hardening and the darkness God's power is displayed and His name proclaimed in all the Earth. The word for proclaimed is *diangello*, a Greek word which means to give notice or to publish, as well as to declare something far and wide. The hardening of the Spirit realm is for the purpose of God's power being declared both in the heavens and in the Earth. Notice that when Pharaoh was hardened it was so that the name of the Lord would be proclaimed *"in all the earth."* It was a national or regional event, but in the spirit realm God was pronouncing to the whole Earth His mastery over natural kings and also over principalities who rule in the dark spirit realm.

c) The hardening will not be reversed because God's purpose requires a final confrontation. God hardened Pharaoh's heart in order to lead towards a climactic battle that would liberate God's people. The system of Babylon represented by Pharaoh is opposed to the Lord and it will never change. It must be judged, found guilty and destroyed. God stands ready to take His vengeance against all the disobedience that has corrupted His Earth since the world began. Two unseen systems are gearing up for an ultimate clash. Therefore the hardening will intensify and grow worse until it is finally judged.

Ancient Egypt was a shadow or a type, but we are living in the day of its substance and fulfillment. Our ancient brothers saw conflict breaking out on every side, but they realized the battles and the increasing hardness was part of the pathway to their ultimate deliverance. We are living in a time of titanic struggle and impending ultimate victory, a fullness of time ordained by God.

Chapter 15
Key Prophetic Similarity #9
Deliverance Comes in the Fullness of Time

The children of Israel were in bondage for 400 years and they prayed and groaned to be liberated from their enslavement. That is 146,000 days over a period of four centuries that people cried out to God for deliverance. But one day, God heard:

> And **now** the cry of the Israelites has reached me, and I have seen the way the Egyptians are oppressing them.
>
> **So now, go.** I am sending you to Pharaoh to bring my people the Israelites out of Egypt."
>
> Exodus 3:9,10

The exit of the Israelites from Ancient Egypt is a prefiguring of the Church of the last days being blasted out of mortality. Our ninth *Key Prophetic Similarity* states that *deliverance comes in the fullness of time*.

We are living in an era when God is dealing with the nations just as He dealt with Ancient Egypt. God was working with many factors which all needed to come to a point of fruition or confluence at one time. One factor was the cry of the people which had accumulated before the Lord over a period of centuries. A second was the preparation of Moses himself. He was a prince groomed in Pharaoh's court with training in politics, economics, the building of store cities and other skills necessary to sustain an empire. God had to break him and strip him of his power, leaving him in the wilderness for forty years. Only then was he finally ready to go back to Pharaoh's palace and be useful to God.

A third factor was the nations that would be judged when Israel came into the Promised Land. The promise to Abraham to inherit the land could not be fulfilled in his own lifetime because *"the sin of the Amorites has not yet reached its full measure"* (Gen 15:15). God was measuring, just like He is measuring Babylon's iniquity which He requires to be paid back double (Rev 18:6). God waited until the Amorites cup of iniquity was full and ready for judgment. Only then could the people of God possess it, so God told Abraham *"In the fourth generation your descendants will come back here"* (Gen 15:16). The nations of Canaan increasing and cumulative wickedness was part of the fullness of time also.

God is patient and merciful. He waits for developments to occur and He never brings judgment prematurely. A good example of that is Methuselah, noted to be the oldest man in the Bible. His name means "after this judgment comes." He was Noah's grandfather and God was looking towards the time when He would judge the whole Earth with a flood.

> *God is patient and merciful; He waits for developments to occur and He never brings judgment prematurely.*

Methuselah died in the year of the flood — God waited and waited to judge the Earth and He ensured the oldest recorded human life passed before He acted. Decades and centuries pass before God finally brings finalization and judgment — but then He does act.

Living in the Season of Fulfillment

But concerning the times and the seasons, brethren, you have no need that I should write to you.

For you yourselves know perfectly that the day of the Lord so comes as a thief in the night.

For when they say, "Peace and safety!" then sudden destruction comes upon them, as labor pains upon a pregnant woman. And they shall not escape.

But you, brethren, are not in darkness, so that this Day should overtake you as a thief.

You are all sons of light and sons of the day. We are not of the night nor of darkness.

1 Thessalonians 5:1-5 (NKJV)

It is plainly stated that no one knows the day or the hour, but it is also authoritatively declared that we *will know* the season of the Lord's return. The coming of the Lord will *not* shock us or catch us unaware or unprepared because we know the time and seasons. For others His coming will be like a thief in the night. A thief doesn't call you up and announce he will be there at 3 am to rob your house. But the day of the Lord does not overtake us as a thief. We are illuminated and aware that we are living in a season of the Lord's soon return.

The translation from mortality to immortality will be a corporate occurrence — we will *all* be released at once at the coming of the Lord. No one knows the day or the hour that this will occur, but this prophetic comparison with ancient Egypt affirms that we are living in the season of the End Times. And it is our responsibility and our spiritual right to know the seasons so we are *"not in darkness, so that this Day should overtake you as a thief. You are all sons of light and sons of the day"* (1 Thess 5:4,5).

Regardless of how long it may take for these events to roll out, we will not be taken by surprise because we are aware that not only is God dealing with the nations but He is making us mature and wise and elevating us to new levels of partnership with Him. We now must move into the final category of the prophetic comparison between Ancient Egypt and Modern America — *The Confrontation.*

Chapter 16
The Man He Imprisons
Cannot be Released

This is the final section of the arc entitled Confrontation. But what is God confronting? Is a natural empire the primary thing God is dealing with when Job said that *"He makes nations great, and destroys them; he enlarges nations, and disperses them"* (Job 12:23)? There is a rise and fall of empire that we can see, but the *Confrontation* is not referring to one political party in conflict with another or a clashing of ideas on how to fix the economy. The *Confrontation* we speak of is much bigger in scope. It is a war in the spirit realm that is breaking out into the natural through crises and destabilization. In talking about the Sovereignty of God in dealing with nations, Job includes another powerful statement:

> *What he tears down cannot be rebuilt; the man he imprisons cannot be released.*
>
> *Job 12:14*

The verse indicates the inevitability of decline, but it also implies that in the decline of a nation there are those who are responsible to the point they can be imprisoned for their guilt in leading the nation to ruin. Clearly this cannot mean a human, the one who happens to hold the reins of power when God tears down the nation, because

> The Confrontation is a war in the spirit realm that is breaking out into the natural through crises and destabilization.

very few of them have ever been imprisoned. There is another, more spiritual application of this verse. God is not only dealing with nations and systems. He is primarily assaulting the spiritual powers behind those systems.

Who is God imprisoning, and who will never be released? It is the devil himself who will be incarcerated forever: *The devil, who deceived them, was thrown into the lake of burning sulfur, where the beast and the false prophet had been thrown. They will be tormented day and night for ever and ever"* (Rev 20:10). His torment will never stop and his imprisonment will be eternal for *"The man He imprisons cannot be released."*

Our warfare is not carnal but spiritual, and we are instructed to fix our eyes on things that can't be discerned in the natural (2 Co 10:2-4, 4:18). We must be careful not to put too great an emphasis on the politicians, economists and leaders in the Earth who are groping about in darkness. Whatever their policies, they are unwitting pawns being moved around the chessboard of a titanic struggle in the spirit realm. The same was true of Pharaoh. When Moses demanded liberation it wasn't just Pharaoh he was talking to — the spiritual powers that kept God's people enslaved had to obey and finally release God's people.

In the natural we see that God is dealing with nations and systems, but beyond that He is going after the spiritual princes behind those systems and that is the primary purpose of the *Confrontation*.

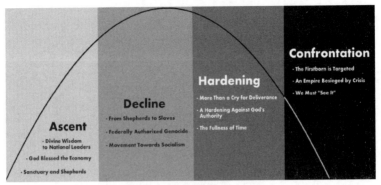

Graphic: Arc 4

The section on Confrontation contains our final three Key Prophetic Similarities:

➤ *Key Prophetic Similarity 10:*
   The Firstborn is Targeted

➤ *Key Prophetic Similarity 11:*
   An Empire Besieged by Crisis

➤ *Key Prophetic Similarity 12:*
   We Must "See It"

The Confrontation has only one possible outcome: the complete victory of Christ over all the principalities and powers and a termination of the enemy's authority to oppress and rule in the Earth realm. The *Confrontation* is God hammering and confronting the spiritual strongholds held by satanic powers and the graphic indicates that the Confrontation is the highest level of God's purpose within the arc — that while the nation is being broken down God is executing His ultimate purpose.

Chapter 17
Key Prophetic Similarity #10
The "Firstborn" is Targeted

We can now state the reason behind the crises. God is targeting the firstborn for destruction, just as he did in Ancient Egypt. Releasing a heavenly attack on the Firstborn of Egypt was part of Moses' prophetic mandate and calling: *"Then say to Pharaoh, 'This is what the LORD says: Israel is my firstborn son, and I told you, "Let my son go, so he may worship me." But you refused to let him go; so I will kill your firstborn son"* (Ex 4:22,23). It is the pitting of God's Firstborn or best against Pharaoh's best in a titanic battle – that is the spiritual origin of all the crises which are striking the Earth.

We see this in the ultimate judgment upon Ancient Egypt, the killing of the firstborn on the night before the Exodus:

> *At midnight the LORD struck down all the firstborn in Egypt, from the firstborn of Pharaoh, who sat on the throne, to the firstborn of the prisoner, who was in the dungeon, and the firstborn of all the livestock as well.*
>
> *Pharaoh and all his officials and all the Egyptians got up during the night, and there was loud wailing in Egypt, for there was not a house without someone dead.*
>
> *Exodus 12:29,30*

The killing of the firstborn was not random judgment or careless genocide. It was strategic and selective.

God targeted every aspect of the empire, from the firstborn of Pharaoh who sat on the throne (the powerful and high social standing), to the firstborn of the

> *The crises today are not accidental or arbitrary; God is targeting the best systems of the earth.*

prisoner (the most marginalized and disempowered of society). No aspect of society was spared. God even killed the firstborn of the livestock (the same metaphor of economic blessing and downturn spoken to a previous Pharaoh in a dream of cattle, Gen 41).

Likewise the crises today are not accidental or arbitrary. We can see how God's sovereign management of the crisis is targeting the best systems of the Earth. For us who live in the era of Modern America, the "firstborn" is the superior nations, systems and expressions of earthly power which are ascendant or which rank as the most important within our global society. This prophetic comparison reveals that at this time in human history God is going after these firstborn systems and nations because the spiritual powers that rule them will not let His Firstborn son go. Let's examine this through looking at two examples: a) "firstborn nations" defined as the world's largest economies b) "firstborn systems" symbolized by the assault on energy.

Firstborn Nations

The United States is the largest single economy in the Earth. If the EU is measured as a whole it becomes number one. We are referring to them as "firstborn nations" because they have the largest and most dominant economies which stood over the nations in the second half of the 20th century. But today both economies are in deep distress. There are 3-4 countries in the Euro zone which could default at any time, dragging the entire continent (and the global economy) down with it. Likewise the U.S. has massive debt and extremely slow economic growth years after the meltdown despite massive government infusions of cash.

These two largest economic blocs in the Earth –"firstborn economies" due to their sheer size and their impact on the rest of the Earth — are in a state of virtual failure. Utilizing the metaphor with Ancient Egypt once again, these nations are like Pharaoh's dream about seven fat cows being eaten by skinny cows. Yet in spite of their enormous consumption they remained sickly. In America and the EU today they have gorged on massive stimulus — trillions in bailouts, quantitative easing, interest rates kept at historic lows — yet these two largest economies remain scrawny, emaciated and vulnerable.

> *The largest or "firstborn" economies are in a state of virtual failure; despite gorging on stimulus they remain scrawny and vulnerable.*

China is the rising empire and is now the second largest economy and it weathered the meltdown a bit better than the developed economies. But if this prophetic comparison is accurate it will also experience economic difficulties, along with other emerging economies in India, Brazil, etc. China seeks to balance growth and stimulus with fears of inflation and they need to keep their factories busy to keep the economy going and their massive population fed and employed. Already there are signs that inflation is creeping and factories have slowed down and the deep tie-in with the wider global economy which has been a source of massive riches, will also prove to be a source of contagion and eventual decline. China's purchase of America's debt to the tune of $1 trillion plus will not serve it well in the future nor will Chinese dependence on America and EU purchasing their manufactured goods — largely on credit. Pharaoh was unable to stop the plagues which shattered his society and he was powerless to prevent the angel of death from strategically selecting and targeting the firstborn in every house. We can expect emerging economies to be targeted also.

Firstborn Systems

The metaphor of the battle of the Firstborn applies not just to nations that are dominant, but also to key systems that are essential for life. One such key system or necessary resource is energy, whether it is coal, oil, natural gas or nuclear energy; all of them have been the focus of divine assault in the last few years. Oil was targeted both in the explosion of the BP oil well Deepwater Horizon in the Gulf of Mexico in 2010, and also via the Arab Spring in 2011 that brought political and social instability in a region which has 60 percent of the world's oil reserves.

Coking coal was hit when floods in Australia covered an area equivalent in size to France and Germany combined in 2010, submerging mines where coking coal is extracted. The coal is essential to the manufacture of steel and the flooding, described as *"a disaster of Biblical proportions"* caused steel prices to rise 30 percent.[8] Australia is also the world's fourth largest supplier of wheat and the floods destroyed one half of the crop. The next month saw the largest increase in food prices since 1974 (food is another key commodity and it will be an important issue moving into the future, as will water).

Finally we have nuclear energy which took a direct hit in the terrible Japanese earthquake in 2011. In addition to killings tens of thousands the disaster traumatized the nation, causing Japanese Prime Minister Naoto Kan to observe *"In the 65 years after the end of World War II, this is the toughest and most difficult crisis for Japan."* The earthquake moved Honshu, Japan's largest island, 7.9 feet east and it

---

[8]Australia flooding of 'biblical proportions' slashes coal, agriculture exports;csmonitor.com/World/Asia-Pacific/2011/0103/Australia-flooding-of-biblical-proportions-slashes-coal-agriculture-exports, retrieved January 25, 2011

shifted the Earth on its axis by nearly 4 inches. It also halted its nuclear energy capability as all nuclear power plants were taken off-line following the breach of Fukushima Daiichi. The assault on the "firstborn" was inadvertently relayed by one journalist reporting on the Japanese tsunami:

"One of the strange things about this disaster is that no place is as well prepared as Japan for this kind of natural disaster. In many respects they have been rehearsing for this for years – in terms of the building standards, in terms of preparedness for tsunamis. But when it struck, it was so violent that **not even the best system in the world (i.e. the firstborn)** *was able to respond sufficiently quickly. It shows just how vulnerable even a country like Japan is to a violent act of nature like this."*[9]

Although he meant it from a totally natural perspective, his words capture what is happening in the spirit realm. God is overwhelming the best systems in the world: a) the biggest economies in the Earth are crippled, deeply indebted and vulnerable b) sophisticated and proven political systems which functioned for hundreds of years are now in gridlock and rendered non-functional c) floods and earthquakes ravage the environment d) man's best engineering can't stop the tsunami or repair an oil well that ruptured a mile beneath the sea's surface e) social and political strife in the Middle East continues more than two years after protests began.

> *God is overwhelming the best systems in the world.*

By the time you read this other crises will have occurred. Clearly God is sending a message and He expects us to discern and hear what He is saying.

---

[9]NBC News Report Ian Williams, reporting by phone from Natori, a coastal town in Japan on March 14, 2011, worldblog.nbcnews.com/?nvo=500&16710058%7Ca%7Cnu%7C30%7C1%7Ct%7Ca%7C500=28, retrieved March 15, 2011

Chapter 18
Key Prophetic Similarity #11
An Empire Besieged by Crisis

Moses was called to be a deliverer and God informed him that the only way for the people to be liberated was through crisis or what God calls "stretching out my hand and striking the Egyptians:"

> *But I know that the king of Egypt will not let you go unless a mighty hand compels him.*
>
> *So I will stretch out my hand and strike the Egyptians with all the wonders that I will perform among them. After that, he will let you go.*
>
> *Exodus 3:19,20*

The word "strike" is the Hebrew word *nakah* and it means just what is says — to attack and destroy, to conquer and subjugate, to send judgment on in order to punish and to kill. However we choose to interpret the word, it's not good news for Ancient Egypt. But it is how God brings judgment on Egypt that is crucial to our understanding — He performs "wonders" among them. The word "wonders" is *pala* and it means to separate or distinguish. The word means to be wonderful and extraordinary, to be surpassing and therefore to separate by distinguishing action. The word also means to be beyond one's power or to be difficult to do.

God is distinguishing Himself as the One who does what no other is capable of, and what no human or spiritual being can stop.

81

God striking Ancient Egypt with wonders was releasing breakage upon society that was beyond the power of the empire to fix or control. It was God separating Himself by surpassing man's ability to govern. They were wonders because God was exerting ultimate control. It was beyond the principalities who seek to lock down people and control life in this realm. He is separating and distinguishing Himself as the One who does what no other is capable of, and what no human or spiritual being can stop. There is a clear sequence spoken by God to Moses. The crises had to come first, because it is only "after that" that Pharaoh will let the people go. Pharaoh is a picture of Satanic powers that rule in the heavenly realm. They keep the people in slavery and have no intention of letting us go. The result is a huge battle in the spirit realm.

Crisis in our Time

The metaphor of Ancient Egypt brings explanation and understanding to what is happening in our time when there is calamity on every side — from economic meltdown to natural disasters to political polarization. Nations scramble to fix them and people have opinions about what must be done, but despite all efforts things continue to get worse. The plagues themselves have a strong parallel for today: a) boils represents disease and the health care system in general which can't keep up with epidemics or costs b) the river being turned to blood represents environmental concerns and natural disasters such as earthquakes, tsunamis, super storms and global warming c) the frogs, lice and locust destroyed crops, thus weakening the nation's economy. The plagues targeted every aspect of a society because it was all constructed not on obedience to God but upon man's wisdom. God is going after the core of rebellion upon which the entire Earth is built — He is punishing the disobedience of the ages through crisis or plagues.

Word of God is Consistent

Other portions of Scripture are in full agreement with the prophetic metaphor of Ancient Egypt as they describe the crises that must come as we move towards the End. Jesus described many aspects of crisis when asked about the end of the age in Matthew 24. Among the events He said would characterize the end:

Massive attempts at deception, *Watch out that no one deceives you. For many will come in my name, claiming, 'I am the Christ,' and will deceive many (v 4,5)*

Unstable international environment, *You will hear of wars and rumors of wars... Nation will rise against nation, and kingdom against kingdom (v 6,7)*

Natural disasters, *There will be famines and earthquakes in various places. (v 7)*

Jesus described a series of crises that will mark our movement towards the end of time which He called signs of the end of the age. He called these things "the beginnings of birth pains," indicating an increasing level of intensity and frequency. This matches Jeremiah's description of the final assault on Babylon. So many crises will happen on top of each other it would be like *"one messenger running to meet another"* with the message that Babylon is surrounded (Jer 51:31). Jeremiah's messengers are CNN, Fox and various media outlets which carry news of the next disaster to the nations. Each "runner" is heralding the collapse of Babylon just as Jeremiah predicted.[10]

And we can't forget Elijah, the prophet of fire who is sent during the *"great and dreadful day of the Lord"* (Mal 4:5). The spirit of Elijah comes during a time of crisis, just as his individual prophetic ministry was the dominant spiritual

---

[10]The entirety of Jeremiah 50 & 51 are prophetic passages that applied to the historic empire of Babylon but also describe in detail how life will be when God launches His final assault against time.

order during a time of economic and political crisis. Elijah purposefully instigated an economic meltdown in the ancient world, shutting off the money supply (rain) to agricultural Israel. He confronted the political realm and he called all of society together to challenge them in a time of moral depravity and spiritual passivity. He called down fire from heaven — he was a prophet of fire who is a symbol of God's movements at the end of the age.

The Word of God is consistent and it describes crisis from many angles: a) Ancient Egypt experiencing plagues; b) Jesus' description of the end of the age; c) Jeremiah's prophetic narrative of the fall of Babylon d) Elijah who stood with prophetic ferocity and crashed Israel's economy.[11] Crisis is the "new normal." This strategic assault will not stop until it accomplishes its purpose. In Egypt it was ten plagues that ratcheted up the stakes until ultimate judgment and deliverance — the killing of the firstborn on the night before liberation. We have to see the crises for what they really are — the final act in God's redemptive work in bringing all things back under His caring and righteous rulership.

---

[11]We will develop these themes from Elijah and Jeremiah 50-51 in future writings.

Chapter 19
Key Prophetic Similarity #12
We Must "See it"

We understand the challenge to the thinking of the Church being put forth in this prophetic comparison. At its core this word is a redefined view of who God is. The children of Israel had the same challenge. Even though they prayed and asked God for deliverance, they didn't understand what Moses was doing and they didn't appreciate the fact that life became more brutal after the first crisis when Pharaoh demanded bricks to be made without straw. Their lack of understanding is revealed when they actually appealed to Pharaoh to keep the conditions of their enslavement as they had been – they wanted to continue to live in "normal" slavery. But Pharaoh had no intention of being reasonable and ordered them "get back to work" under the more harsh conditions (Ex 5:15-18).

It was a spiritual struggle, a conflict which revolved around the ability to perceive what God was doing. Darkness never wants us to know and Pharaoh, a symbol of Satanic principalities, told the Israelites that they should *"keep working and pay no attention to lies"* (Ex 5:9). Moses spoke for God and declared it was a day of deliverance, but Pharaoh called the word from God "lies" that should be dismissed. As we pray and consider how God wants us to understand, we can learn from two issues the Israelites had to work through in order to come to a place of accurate prophetic sight.

A) Wrong concepts about God

May the Lord look upon you and judge you! (Ex 5:21)

The people Moses was sent to deliver were so upset they told him God would judge him for what he had done. At the core of their misperception was a view that God would never do something like initiate crisis. They had a wrong concept of God. They wanted Moses to be judged by God because they (incorrectly) perceived what he'd done wasn't the will of God. It is worth noting that their response to the crisis was in contradiction to their own prayers and groanings for deliverance. Clearly they were confused and had limited understanding that made them oppose what they had previously asked God for.

At the core of their misperception about God was that He wouldn't bring crisis that disrupted life, very much like today where incorrect definitions of

> *The ramping up of crisis is not an act of cruelty; it is the ultimate act of mercy and redemption.*

"grace" compel Christians to wrongly believe that God would never bring judgment or crisis. The people of God lived in slavery and had no explanation for all the hardship. It is obvious they didn't have a developed way of thinking about their suffering and their conceptual view of God was limited. How could they be upset at Moses for initiating crisis, but not explain why they were enslaved in the first place? It is the same in our day when people protest that God would never bring judgment, but they also have no coherent explanation for all the suffering that takes place within the realm of mortality in which we live. If we lack a correct view of God and His Sovereignty we won't have an explanation for the crisis.

We have to be very clear about the fact that God's heart is always redemptive. The ramping up of crisis in the

Earth is not an act of cruelty by a heartless God who doesn't care how many are crushed by crisis. It is the ultimate act of mercy and redemption. Yes, people are dying in tsunamis and suffering in famine — every one of them precious to God. He has demonstrated His love and care for every human in that *"while we were yet sinners Christ died for us"* (Rom 5:8). There are individual events or agents of death, tragic things like tsunamis, earthquakes, cancer, etc. and God, who notes even when a sparrow falls to the ground and who has already paid the ultimate price for redemption, notes every human's death and suffering.

But this strategic assault is going after something even bigger than these agents of death — God is going after Death itself. Death has claimed every human life since time began and God's assault on Death through crisis comes from His heart of redemption and care.[12] Like a woman experiencing increasingly intense birth pangs, pain is the only way through to abundant life and ultimate blessing. Once the birth pangs begin they don't stop until delivery; there is no reverse gear. God will *"Swallow up death forever, And the Lord GOD will wipe away tears from all faces; He will remove the disgrace of His people from all the earth"* (Is 25:8). The crisis is not to initiate suffering, but to bring final deliverance from pain…forever!

B) Responding From an Emotional Basis

You have made us a stench to Pharaoh and his officials and have put a sword in their hand to kill us. (Ex 5:21)

A second incorrect response by the people was to view the crisis from an emotional basis. They were afraid of the hardship and they thought Pharaoh would kill them because of the move towards deliverance. They didn't understand that the crisis and difficulty was a part of a larger sequence of events that had to take place that was part of

---

[12]Two men did not die; Enoch and Elijah are types for the last day Church which is destined to rise up and overcome death.

His fulfillment of His covenant with Abraham. God had promised Abraham,

"Then the LORD said to him, "Know for certain that your descendants will be strangers in a country not their own, and they will be enslaved and mistreated four hundred years.

But I will punish the nation they serve as slaves, and afterward they will come out with great possessions."

Genesis 15:13,14

Within the statement to Abraham we see a clearly defined series of events: a) massive immigration into a strange land b) servitude, hardship and oppression for an ordained period c) movement to judgment of Ancient Egypt d) eventual release from the bondage e) overwhelming blessing for God's people. It was a series of events that had to occur in a clear divine sequence. One part cannot be selected out over the others. One cannot opt for the overwhelming blessing at the end without embracing the requirement to successfully walk

> *An emotional response would get in the way of God's intent to judge evil and set you free and bring you into immortality.*

through the conditions of life in Ancient Egypt. It is a non-negotiable, all inclusive package which cannot be customized for personal comfort or preference.

What this means is that if you were an Israelite in Ancient Egypt at the time of God's judgment and you saw all of the destruction, wreckage and suffering taking place around you, your first impulse might be to pray for the terrible events of the time to stop. But to do so you would actually be praying and asking God to break His ancient covenant with Abraham. An emotional response would get in the way of God's expressed intent to judge evil, set you free and bring you into immortality. Any prayer that effectively asks God to go back on His word, not to judge the evil in the world's system and goes counter to His intent to bring blessing, will be ultimately ineffective and will not be heard by God.

But if you knew that what was taking place was a divine sequence that would lead to God's judgment of evil and deliverance and freedom for His people, then your prayer changes. Your sight and response to the disasters around you change because within it you see God's hand of ultimate redemption. What would bring despair to an Ancient Egyptian brings hope to you because you know the divine sequence and the eventual outcome which have been sealed and made certain by covenant many years before the crisis began.

This is where the people of God need to stand in the midst of God's confrontation of the systems of oppression in the Earth. We can be encouraged that our ancient brothers confronted the false perspectives that tried to distort their view of what God was doing. By the end of the process the entire nation of Israel was keenly aware of what was happening. Each one sat in their home as the angel of death swept through the land. They painted blood on their doorposts and dressed for a quick exit because they knew the meaning of the crisis. They had come to a place of understanding that the destruction was of God and it was redemptive.

Before Going Any Further...

Chapter 20
Responding to the Prophetic Word

A word from God is a powerful thing. No man can force God to talk, but when He does speak we must respond. The voice of God can't be ignored, minimized or played around with. God proclaims Himself in the Earth and we are expected to align with what He is saying. A declaration from heaven does not come over and stand by us while we casually consider if it fits into the structure of our lives. The Kingdom does not accommodate man. Instead we have to make room for His Kingdom in our hearts and lives.

God requires us to respond when He speaks. He commands us to *"Give ear, O my people, to my law; Incline your ears to the words of my mouth"* (Ps 78:1). The word incline means to bend or turn towards, and we have to turn our hearts and bend our minds towards "the words of His mouth." We have finished Part 2 detailing the word of the Lord that *Modern America is like Ancient Egypt*, and we have to pause and consider our response. We want to ensure that we posture ourselves to hear and receive what God is saying.

We know this is not an easy word to hear, especially for those of us who are believers in America. Some questions may have popped into your mind as you read such as: a) What about the nation being restored? b) Could all the crisis and difficulty *really* be God's purpose? We have to work through these questions in order to correctly hear this word from God. The first question is based in our personal desires, preferences, beliefs and convictions — especially regarding America. The second reflects our understanding of who God is, because this prophetic metaphor challenges our concepts about God Himself.

What do we do about these questions? Thankfully, we have a clear Biblical example to guide us as we consider how to respond to this word. These are the same key issues that surfaced when Jesus and the disciples contended with the purposes of God that led to intense crisis in the Garden of Gethsemane and the cross, events which form a template for our response to this word from God.

Jesus and the Disciples in the Garden

Nothing in the disciples was ready for Jesus to die on the cross. The disciples were shocked at the turn of events and at one point Peter took Jesus aside to tell Him the cross must not happen. Jesus responded with a

> *No one wants to see the nation destabilized; if given a choice, we would all choose restoration.*

strong rebuke towards Peter, identifying his sentiment as coming from the dark spirit realm: *"He rebuked Peter. 'Get behind me, Satan!' He said. 'You do not have in mind the things of God, but the things of men'"* (Mk 8:33). Strong emotional desires, even loyalty and love for that which is good, can be used by the enemy to withstand God's purpose. The personal desires and beliefs of the disciples caused them to take up swords in the garden and fight to keep Jesus from being arrested, but they were fighting against God's purpose.

No one wants to see the nation destabilized. If given a choice between crisis and breakdown on the one hand and a return to a much better time of America's past on the other, we would all choose restoration. Intense desire, passion and strong personal preferences must be laid aside in order to discern the will of God. We don't always get our preferences and can learn from Jesus' sorrow and agony in the garden. Jesus had to wrestle with His personal desires also. He didn't want to suffer and He asked the Father to take the cup from Him, but realized it was the will of the Lord to endure the agony and He embraced it.

The second and even more substantial objection to this word from God is our concept of who God is. Could He really be using darkness and crisis to deal with the Earth? In fact Jesus recognized that was God's plan. When He was arrested by the soldiers his disciples tried to fight, but Jesus said *"This is your hour — when darkness reigns"* (Lu 22:53). What an incredible statement! Jesus understood that darkness hates God, but in the realm of God's complete and total Sovereignty in which He is over ALL THINGS, even darkness works for His purpose. Today in America is very much like the events in the garden — Darkness has not only made inroads into society, but it is largely prevailing. It is the hour when Darkness is reigning in the nation, but we should not be horrified or broken because the Darkness is accomplishing the will of God.

Darkness reigned in Ancient Egypt as plague after plague destroyed society, but God used it to blast His people out of bondage and bring them into the Promised Land. Darkness thought it was winning when it murdered the Son of God, but that dark hour stands as the high point of redemption within human history. And now Darkness is ravaging the Earth as people suffer under the heavy yoke of economic meltdown, natural disasters and increasing social slide towards immorality and brokenness. Darkness is reigning now but God has a purpose and He will triumph!

We can respond to this word from God the same way the disciples responded to Jesus going to the cross. We can reject it, fight against it and declare that it is not God's will for crisis to strike America, but it will only lead to us being like the disciples who were confused, broken and scattered. We must learn from Jesus' response to the cross and to the overwhelming push of Darkness which unleashed itself against Him. He walked through the crisis and massive redemption was experienced. Put in such stark comparison we will all choose to respond as Jesus did and there are

> *The crisis in the garden was a fulfillment of God's purpose and Jesus knew it and let it continue even thought he had the power to stop it.*

three platforms we can see working within Jesus as He dealt with the crisis: a) don't let the crisis de-activate you b) recognize that my obedience is a link in an unbroken chain of God's purpose c) refuse to take up the sword.

a) Don't Allow Crisis De-activate You

And being in anguish, he prayed more earnestly, and his sweat was like drops of blood falling to the ground.

When he rose from prayer and went back to the disciples, he found them asleep, exhausted from sorrow.

"Why are you sleeping?" he asked them. "Get up and pray so that you will not fall into temptation."

Luke 22:44-46

The Bible describes Jesus as *"deeply distressed and troubled,"* and that His *"soul is overwhelmed with sorrow to the point of death"* (Mk 14:33,34). The words describe being alarmed and afraid. It is ok if we have a desire not to go through the crises — Jesus asked the Father to allow the cup to pass from Him, calling on God's limitless possibilities and options, but ultimately He surrendered to the will of the Lord. Jesus knew it was the Father's will for Him to be betrayed, arrested and crucified.

In response to the agony and anguish of the crisis Jesus *"prayed more earnestly."* His command to the disciples was to pray so they wouldn't surrender to the pressures and difficulty of the trying times, but they fell asleep, exhausted from sorrow. They were not physically exhausted. They fell asleep because they couldn't bear up under the weight of the spiritual pressure. The crisis deactivated them spiritually. The experience of Jesus and the disciples in the garden teaches us that if we don't pray more earnestly we *will be* overwhelmed with sorrow because the burden is too great.

We cannot be asleep spiritually at this time, neutered by the intensity of the spirit realm which is increasingly bearing down upon humanity. We must bear up under the load. We have to remain engaged in the spirit realm, praying and having a rich and spiritually fertile internal life that remains strong as the weight of the crisis increases. God's global movements against the principalities which manifest in the Earth as crisis cannot deactivate us and we cannot be made spiritually passive or become exhausted by sorrow. We have a responsibility to present a spiritual standard to God. The need is for an active and highly developed spiritual life that has been cultivated and built within our internal man over a period of time. We have to be spiritually engaged in the midst of hostility. Our prayers and engagement with God must intensify as the times grow darker.

> *His command to the disciples was to pray so they wouldn't surrender to the pressures and difficulty of the trying times.*

b) Recognize that My Obedience is a Link in an Unbroken Chain of God's Purpose

In that hour Jesus said to the crowd, "Am I leading a rebellion, that you have come out with swords and clubs to capture me? Every day I sat in the temple courts teaching, and you did not arrest me.

But this has all taken place that the writings of the prophets might be fulfilled." *Then all the disciples deserted him and fled.*

> ***But this has all taken place that the writings of the
> prophets might be fulfilled.*** *"Then all the disciples de-
> serted him and fled.*
>
> *Matthew 26:55,56*

The crisis in the garden was a fulfillment of God's
purpose and Jesus knew it and let it continue even though
He had the power to stop it. The difficulty of the cross was
made bearable because Jesus was aware He was standing at
the point of fulfillment. He remained calm and resolute
while those without sight were broken and scattered. Jesus said He must fulfill all that the prophets had spoken.
His life was constrained and He chose to honor the words
of his brothers spoken down through the centuries. He saw
His life — and His death — as fitting within a flow of
events that had been ordained by the Lord and He chose
to submit to the bigger plan of heaven.

The disciples deserted him and fled because they
didn't understand God's redemptive purpose was being
worked out right before their eyes. They saw their lives
only in the immediate circumstances of crisis: betrayal, arrest, crucifixion, etc. We have to see the bigger picture that
goes far beyond my immediate circumstances and even
transcends my lifetime. God has been setting up the nations to fulfill His purpose since the beginning of time, and
we are now living at the end-point of His purpose. Huge
macro purposes are coming to pass in our time. Our individual lives and destinies fit within those big tectonic plates
that are shifting around in the spirit realm. Economies are
falling, nations are becoming more darkened and society
is on a trajectory that will result in ultimate judgment.

We can't say to God "no" because we are uncomfortable or
afraid. The events have been set in
motion and they are ordained to
happen. If we don't understand

> *It is not the will of
> God for us to be bro-
> ken, confused, scattered
> and stripped naked as
> the disciples were.*

and reject the will of God, then like the disciples we will be bruised and battered by the very things God has arranged to bring fulfillment to His plan. We must align ourselves with what God is doing in the Earth and not oppose Him by trying to avoid the crisis or restore something He has ordained to fracture. If we do, we will be broken and flee — we will be unnecessarily hammered by processes and events God has set in motion that cannot be stopped.

c) Refuse to Take up the Sword

Then Simon Peter, who had a sword, drew it and struck the high priest's servant, cutting off his right ear. (The servant's name was Malchus.) Jesus commanded Peter, "Put your sword away! Shall I not drink the cup the Father has given me?"

John 18:10

The soldiers arrested Jesus and Peter took out his sword and cut off an ear. Jesus commanded Peter to put his sword away but He gave no such command to the soldiers. Malchus, whose name comes from the Greek word for "king," represents government authority. The government was unjust when they arrested and crucified Christ because He was perfectly innocent. Yet God utilized the injustice of the state to fulfill His redemptive plan, just as He is using the dysfunctionality and destabilization of modern government policy for His purpose.

> *The temptation is to first respond to the crisis out of our natural strength, but these actions are not based in faith and they will not prevail.*

Like Peter, many sincere and devoted followers of Christ today rise up in zeal to resist governmental authority. They believe a primary issue is the strength of America's political heritage, which is being ruined and if it can be restored the nation would be righted. They will engage in things like legal challenges to federal/state authority, militia movements that reject existing government institutions and seek instead to build alternate societies or states threatening secession from the federal union, etc. Not all who do these things will be believers, but there will be a strong representation of evangelical Christians who are involved in these movements or who are sympathetic to these views.

But Jesus said plainly that he wasn't leading a rebellion against the government and that statement is still true. The temptation is to first respond to the crisis out of our natural strength. Things like hoarding money or fleeing the nation or perhaps even joining a militia movement. But these actions are not based in faith — they all originate in human strength and they will not prevail. If we live by the sword we will die by it also — these movements will not produce the fruit of righteousness any more than Peter cutting off an ear that was quickly repaired by the Lord Himself.

Only That Which is of Christ can Overcome

*Then **everyone deserted him and fled.***

*A young man, wearing nothing but a linen garment, was following Jesus. When they seized him, **he fled naked, leaving his garment behind.***
Mark 14:50,51

The disciples were committed and sincere. They were called to be apostles and they were in an intense discipleship process. They had followed Jesus for 3+ years. They had left their jobs, traveled around Judea and interacted intimately with the Son of God, receiving His teachings and seeing miracles. They had been sent as teams into the villages where Jesus Himself was planning to go — they were used by God for strategic purpose. They were misunderstood by the religious establishment, but they followed Him and stood with Him in every situation — until the Garden. When the crisis hit, *everyone* deserted him and fled. The only one who stood resolutely in the crisis was Christ Himself.

We are like the disciples and their brokenness must be a lesson for us. We have sincerely followed and have shown our devotion to God in many ways, being sent on missions and interacting with the Lord intimately. We have seen miracles and had our lives redirected by the Lord. It is *not* the will of God for us to be broken, confused, scattered and stripped naked as they were. But unless we are more fully formed into Christ's image and likeness we will be just like the disciples. The need is for the Church to move into a massive process of transformation because movement towards Christ is our only place of refuge.

This prophetic word is not primarily informational. It is a summons from God, a call to the Church to come into full Christ-likeness as He always intended. We have to be engaged in a process of on-going transformation that brings us into heightened levels of maturity and awareness so that when we see Darkness all around us we say "all these things must happen"

> *This prophetic word is a summons from God, a call to the Church to come into full Christ-likeness as He always intended.*

with full confidence that God is managing the process. We have to answer the following questions:

- ✔ What is the process of transformation that must occur in my life?

- ✔ How does God expect me to live now that I have this knowledge?

- ✔ What does every church and believer need to know in order to stand strong in a time of crisis?

- ✔ How must I build my marriage and my home in this vital time of God's dealings with the Earth?

- ✔ What key issues is God emphasizing and focusing on in our personal development and what are the necessary processes that will bring us to the point of readiness?

We want to be made into the people of God who rejoice in crisis and stand in our houses filled with worship and awe on the night when the angel of death killed the firstborn of every house in Ancient Egypt. We have to know the processes that transformed our brothers, a process that took them from being a bunch of slaves and made them into a powerful nation ready for exit. These are the critical questions we turn our attention to as we move into part 3 of this book, where we will examine the Partnership God is building with His people.

Part 3

TRANSFORMATION AND OUR ULTIMATE DESTINY

Chapter 21
Arise and Shine!

We have looked at what God was doing with the empire during the progression of the arc. But now we want to look at what God is doing in His people, the Church:

> *Arise, shine, for your light has come, and the glory of the LORD rises upon you.*
>
> *See, darkness covers the earth and thick darkness is over the peoples, but the LORD rises upon you and his glory appears over you.*
>
> *Nations will come to your light, and kings to the brightness of your dawn.*
>
> Isaiah 60:1-3

In a time of great darkness (crisis in the nations), it is time for the Church to shine more brightly than ever before. The Hebrew word for darkness is

> *It is during the time of dark conditions in the nations when God releases light and glory in the Church.*

choshek and it means destruction, death, ignorance, sorrow and wickedness. Gross darkness is a different word, *araphel*, and it literally means to droop or drip down to the lowest level. It describes the misery and gloom of those who don't know God in a time of intense crisis. It is during the time of dark conditions in the nations when God releases light and glory in the Church.

This matches what was happening in Ancient Egypt with the Israelites. While God was breaking the external structures of Ancient Egypt, He was transforming the people of Israel. In the midst of the blindness and destabilization in wider society, the people of God were coming into increasing light, illumination and spiritual sight. As it was then, it is the crises which received all the headlines and drew the nation's attention. But there were powerful spiritual movements that were hidden and unknown to Ancient Egypt. No one took notice of it. It did not come with spectacular occurrences or attract news headlines. Its drama did not play itself out in outer events, but rather on the inside of people's hearts and minds as they were made ready by God to exit Ancient Egypt and journey into a new future with Him.

> *Then the angel of God, who had been traveling in front of Israel's army, withdrew and went behind them.*
>
> *The pillar of cloud also moved from in front and stood behind them, coming between the armies of Egypt and Israel.* ***Throughout the night the cloud brought darkness to the one side and light to the other side; so neither went near the other all night long.***
>
> *Exodus 14:19,20*

God was dismantling Egypt through successive crises, while at the same time He was building and maturing His people, getting them ready for exit from Ancient Egypt. He was preparing them for a journey with Him towards the Promised Land. This is a dramatic picture of dual divine intent inside the account of Israel's departure from Egypt. It lets us know that where God's judgment, destruction and darkness were operating, there was also light, sanctuary and salvation being released to the people of God. Both the darkness (crisis and destabilization) and the light (intense spiritual resource and protection) were being managed by God. These realities can be seen in the graphic below:

Graphic: Arc 5

The graphic portrays that at the most intense level of crisis is also the time of God's greatest resourcing of His people. The Church has been advancing and progressing throughout the entire spectrum of the arc, growing in Christ-likeness as God restores truths and eternal realities within His Body. While the empire is at a low point we are ascendant. As Babylon splinters and fractures we are being built comprehensively by God's Spirit. Each side had a different process. If you asked an Egyptian what God did through the crisis, he would tell you that He devastated their empire and violently tore them to pieces. If you asked an Israelite, he would declare that God gave him hope, a new identity, deliverance and a future. It is this second component, the nature of Israel's experience that this section focuses on.

Transformation Imperatives

The book is entitled *Exodus* because it is the story of how God brings a people out of one dimension of life into another. The narrative describes one of the most powerful transformations in human history and it reveals the lengths that God is going to *in our day* to raise up a people for Himself.

All around us is economic meltdown, natural disasters and political dysfunction. God is doing His part — He is striking the systems with crises and in the Spirit realm a prophetic declaration of "let my people go!" is resounding through the corridors of Darkness. In the environment of ever intensifying crisis God's people became stronger, more filled with faith and into a greater place of partnership with God and His purposes. We have to engage with what we call *Transformation Imperatives* — an imperative is an unavoidable requirement.

There are 7 *Transformation Imperatives* that we will look at from the Word of God. They tell the story of a nation of slaves, a people who were beat down for 400 years and were weak and lacking in spiritual sight. But they changed and the story of their transformation must become our possession also. Their journey is recorded so we could discover and implement the same spiritual principles they accessed from God.

Making it Our Possession

But it isn't only ancient history that will unfold in these pages. These *Transformation Imperatives* are also the story of Congress WBN, the Kingdom entity that began as an apostolic network in 1993 (*www.congresswbn.org/about/*). Don't be confused by the name "Congress WBN." When most of us hear the word we immediately think of the government in Washington, DC but that is not what we mean. We chose the name Congress because the word has two meanings, both of which fit what God has done and is doing with us.

The first meaning of "congress" is that it is a deliberative body that governs. As we experienced the move toward greater Kingdom life, this meaning best captured our commitment to bring the rule of God to our lives and churches and also to influence wider spheres of life on whatever level God would empower us to so do. The word "congress" is also a verb meaning to move closer and closer together, to assemble together and to come to a place of oneness. The oneness captured by the word "congress" describes not only the strong and cohesive nature of our relationships, but also the ability to build that which is coherent and able to move as one man across a planet that is filled with diverse cultures, nationalities and ethnicities.

In our early days we were known as World Breakthrough Network, one of the apostolic networks that began to proclaim the Apostolic Reformation and work closely with churches in the early days of this current move of God. God helped us and He joined to us many who had a hunger and desire to break out of their limited religious structures. In the intervening 20 years we expanded into 95 nations and now work with hundreds of church communities and thousands of people. Beyond the churches, we have been able to leverage Kingdom influence into many areas of life including education, the business/professional/economic realm, political realities and technology initiatives.

We recognize that anything built within us is ultimately from the Lord. If it is just human effort, then those who build labor in vain and they will be rejected even though they did powerful work for God (Ps 127:1, Mt 7:21). God has been faithful to build within us the principles and spiritual realities we write about in this section. It has been a journey of two decades of consistent upward growth and development. God has been with us and helped us to the point that the things we are writing about in this section are not just teachings or principles from the Word of God, they are also realities that have been built within thousands of individual lives and hundreds of church communities. People living in America and in 95 nations are a testament to the faithfulness of

God to work with a broken and scattered people and to form them into a cohesive company.

In that sense these *Transformation Imperatives* are both a series of spiritual principles and teachings from the Bible, but they are also a relational resource, offered in humility and in obedience to the command *"freely you have received, freely give"* (Mt 10:8). We will share specific aspects of our development in the chapters ahead, both the challenges and stimulants to growth we experienced and also lessons learned in our corporate migration.

How you read Part 3 is important. You may want to go through it the first time to simply read and get an overview. But each chapter has within it a density that can be studied and thoughtfully applied within each individual life. In addition, we provide questions that can be considered as each reader thinks about their own transformation process. You can find those at *www.arcofempires.org/interact.*

As you revisit the chapters, you can go into the spiritual depth that is contained within each chapter and also take advantage of the questions we provide on the website. As you apply the principles to your own life circumstances, the power of the Word of God will unfold and you will become more equipped and Christ-like, able to shine in the midst of the darkness of the crisis.

Chapter 22
We Are All Enslaved

When we think of slavery our minds immediately jump to the jagged scar that runs across America's soul caused by the 400 year enslavement of Africans. In more recent days the sex slave trade has proliferated as people, most of them women, are taken against their will and forced into prostitution to enrich those who ruthlessly exploit them. No matter where and how it has manifested, slavery is terrible and oppressive, which makes it all the more remarkable when we consider that the enslavement of the Israelites was arranged by God Himself.

The enslavement of the Israelites was not just an accident of history or the result of the recurring cycles of one nation oppressing weaker people for economic gain. God sent Joseph and then his whole family down to Ancient Egypt, causing a famine that forced them to relocate and eventually be enslaved. The Lord could have just as easily prospered the farmers of Canaan and given them insight to store up grain for a coming famine to ensure His people had food. He did not do that because He wanted the Israelites enslaved and locked down, groaning in their oppression and in need of powerful deliverance. It was His choice to leave them there for 400 years before initiating a series of crises to break them out which He describes in detail.

God ensured the entire Exodus was recorded in the Bible for all of humanity to read and understand in order to receive spiritual life, illumination and wisdom. Given that all this was done by a Sovereign God who never makes a mistake and always has a deeper meaning behind everything He does, we can only draw one conclusion — in God's mind the context of slavery is relevant to us all.

The Fall Enslaved us All

This word from God is powerful not just because it describes what is happening in the nations with crisis but even more so because it captures the real issue lying behind the destabilization, which is to break God's people out of slavery to mortality. The metaphor continues to apply very powerfully in this section, because if mortality is indeed an oppressive master then we are all enslaved.

The Fall of Adam described in the book of Genesis plunged all mankind into a state not intended for us by God. Consider the language and words God uses in Genesis 3 to describe the new reality in which Adam and Eve found themselves as a result of what they had done. They suggest that their fallen state (which the Bible teaches we were all born into as a result) is defined by oppression, domination and suffering. From the New King James version we see words such as "sorrow," "pain," "cursed" and "toil." We see statements from God such as "thorns and thistles the earth will bring forth for you," "from the sweat of your face you shall eat bread" and most devastatingly, "God drove out the man" [from the Garden of Eden]. The language paints a picture of a fall into bondage and suffering. Adam's sin plunged him into a new fallen reality which changed the nature of his existence and experience on Earth. God's opinion of this reality is summed up when He said "cursed is the ground."

The thing about slavery is that the trauma that comes with it is always experienced most by the one who is taken into slavery as compared with the one born as a slave.

> *Adam once lived in a world where he had complete and unrestricted access to the mind of God.*

The one taken into slavery knows the freedom that he has lost. He has a contrasting point of reference which accentuates his sense of loss and pain. In this regard, I imagine that Adam was the only man to be able to truly understand in literal terms the horror of living in mortality. After all, he once lived in a dimension where God would walk with him every day. He once lived in a world where he had complete and unrestricted access to the mind of God. He once functioned in seamless partnership with God to bring order to the Earth. He once stood as a king under God, ruling and governing all that God had created. Nothing can compare to this.

Even though this world does offer us many beautiful things, moments and experiences and even though we can live full lives here, if you describe to Adam the fullest, most beautiful human life, he would say that it pales in comparison to what he had before. Nothing in this Earth would fill the void left in Adam's life by being torn away from a life with God. If you ask Adam to describe life here in Time, he would say it is like slavery to an oppressive master. And if you ask him what his overwhelming desire is, it would be to be free to return home to the place where God had ordained him to live and rule with Him.

The problem for those born as slaves is that unlike Adam, they have no experience to which to compare it. Slavery is all they have ever known and as a result it is easier for them to live in and accept the life it offers even though it is way below where God intended them to be. This is the position that all men born after Adam found themselves in, including us. As difficult as it might be for some of us to believe, life here in this Earth is in fact the result of a fall (a descent; a collapse; a decrease). It simply cannot compare to our ordained place of dwelling with God. But we cannot know this by experience, only by faith in what the word of God tells us.

For those born in slavery to the conditions of the fall, it is easier for us to become satisfied with the things that this life offers to us. It becomes easier to give our all in pursuing the pleasures of this world. Soon the slavery system starts to tell us who we are and we wholeheartedly accept it because without the word of God, there is no countervailing voice telling us otherwise. We become who the system tells us to become. It gives us our values, aspirations, hopes and dreams. And without realizing it, we end up living a false, "happy life" in a system that has in fact enslaved us and thinking that pig's food is a king's feast. It is this state of deception and blanket of darkness that has come to rest upon all humanity that God intends to smash and destroy. In this regard, we are the Israelites enslaved in Ancient Egypt. We live in bondage to Time, separated from our Father who is in eternity. And the only way in which we will ever be released is through a violent spiritual confrontation of this system of slavery by God.

The Destructive Nature of Slavery

For Israel, 400 years was a long time to have been in slavery. The success of slavery as a system depended upon the systematic destruction of anything that would result in social cohesion and unified identity among the slaves. This was done deliberately to prevent mobilization of any sort by the slaves against those who oppressed them. As a result, families were broken up, tribes were separated and people who spoke the same language were kept separated. Over the years this fragmented state conditioned destructive attitudes towards family life and community living.

Slavery forced people into a type of individual survival mode which destroyed their capacity for community life. It created a tendency to reflexively think about ourselves first rather than others. This same fragmentation, division, self-focus and absence of corporate identity associated with the effects of slavery can be seen in the Church as a result of our enslavement to this fallen world.

It is no wonder that in Ephesians 4:13, the stated reason for the fivefold ministry is to bring the Church to the "unity of the faith." This divine intent implies that the Church is splintered and needs to be put back together again. The system of this world has created divisions and schisms within the Body of Christ so as to maintain our subjugated position and to prevent our mobilization to depart and get back to God. Dealing with this division is so critical that it is the very purpose of the fivefold ministry.

The Church Must Groan

God is moving in the Earth to liberate His people but His desire to free us must be met with the desire within the Church to be set free. We saw this in Israel when God was moved to act because the groaning of the enslaved came before Him. There must be a righteous discontent with our current state of life in Time and on Earth. We must see its limitations and its restrictions for what they are. We must feel the burden that Time has placed upon us and we must desire freedom unto Him more than anything else.

Consider the words of Paul in 2 Corinthians 5:1-9 (NKJV):

For we know that if our earthly house, this tent, is destroyed, we have a building from God, a house not made with hands, eternal in the heavens.

For in this we groan, *earnestly desiring to be clothed with **our habitation which is from heaven**,* *if indeed, having been clothed, we shall not be found naked.*

For we who are in this tent groan, being burdened, *not because we want to be unclothed, but further clothed, that mortality may be swallowed up by life.*

Now He who has prepared us for this very thing is God, who also has given us the Spirit as a guarantee.

So we are always confident, knowing that **while we are at home in the body we are absent from the Lord.**

For we walk by faith, not by sight.

We are confident, yes, well pleased rather to be absent from the body and to be present with the Lord. Therefore we make it our aim, whether present or absent, **to be well pleasing to Him.**

Clearly Paul thought of this life in mortality as imprisonment. His words remind us of the account of the Israelites in Egypt and their groaning to which God responded. Paul was speaking here to the church at Corinth which was filled with believers who disappointingly had very carnal lives and pursuits. For example, he indicated in 1 Cor. 5:1 that there were reports of sexual immorality among them that were not even reported among the Gentiles. They pursued material things, did not love one another and had a dysfunctional community life. They were bogged down by desires, attitudes and lifestyle patterns that did not come from God but from the Earth. The Holy Spirit gave Paul, as an apostle, the ability to write the Corinthians the Word of the Lord in order to cultivate within them an appetite for a life beyond this Earth. He describes living here in Time as burdensome and likened it to being naked and not fully dressed.

The example of the Corinthians lets us know that the process of being set free physically is different from the process of being set free in mentality and lifestyle. Any sociologist or historian who has studied the effects of slavery would bear this out. Abolishing slavery is one thing. Getting the slave to think and act as a free man is an entirely different thing altogether. The believers in Corinth had been set free through the power of salvation, but still engaged in behaviors that demonstrated their continued enslavement to the things of this world. The role of their apostolic leader was to reorient their minds and get them to desire their "habitation which is from heaven" and to see the misery of life in mortality so that they stopped desiring it.

> *Abolishing slavery is one thing. Getting the slave to think and act as a free man is an entirely different thing altogether.*

Slavery changes people in very deep and fundamental ways — from personality to outlook on life and self. Coming out of slavery requires both a physical departure and a mental departure. The latter is much harder than the first and takes much longer but it must be done. This is what it was like for Israel when Moses arrived on the scene to declare that the time of their deliverance was at hand. This is what it is like for all of us who were born here enslaved in time, separated from our Father. This is what it is like for those who are now living in the day when the Lord is proclaiming that His deliverance is at hand as He confronts the systems of the Earth to set us free. We must get ready for departure so that divine initiative will one day intersect gloriously with human readiness.

Make no mistake. This prophetic word is not primarily informational merely trying to get us to understand that one empire is very much like another. It is a summons from God. He is calling from Heaven and His voice is thundering in the Earth in order to wake His people up. The Spirit of God is speaking into our spiritual ears with the declaration "it is time to change!" And the Holy Spirit is our Helper, the One who comes close to us to guide us towards greater Christ-likeness. The prophetic metaphor which unfolded as we compared Modern America to Ancient Egypt now comes to life as we consider our enslavement within mortality and God's intention to break us out of Time and bring us into Eternity to rule with Him forever.

As we read through this section we are meant to discover what it means to groan for a fuller life with God. The chapters which detail the *Transformation Imperatives* are not quick fixes no more than a slave can internally become a free man in one day. They will require consistent obedience, effort, commitment and desire. Like the Israelites, they require that we respond to God. The message of the Exodus is that there can be no freedom without the human responsibility to hear, obey and change. We have to embrace the responsibility to participate in the process towards our own liberation by being transformed by the renewing of our minds from slaves to sons of God. Our transformation in Christ is our warfare in this the Last Days. It is the ultimate groan we can lift up to God from within Time.

Chapter 23
Searching it Out

Crime detective shows are all the rave today. One of the more popular and successful of these types of shows comsing out of the U.S. is the "Law & Order" franchise. It is remarkable to see how the detectives are able to start off with so little, but by the end of the show they are able to solve the crime through thorough investigation and deductive reasoning. The investigative process tells us that small clues can tell big stories if you know how to listen carefully to what they have to say. It is an approach that is very relevant as we begin Part 3 of this book.

The reason why this approach is relevant for us is because most of the Biblical account in Exodus is about the devastation wreaked upon Ancient Egypt by the word of the Lord through Moses. By contrast, the impact upon Israel brought about by having to walk through a plague-ridden Egypt is

> *God delights in people who seek Him and pursue His knowledge and wisdom.*

not always spelled out for us in clear and detailed terms. In looking at the crises we gaze upon the Sovereignty of God and His power. But in examining how God's people responded to His initiative, we have to investigate the human side of the process towards liberation.

God delights in people who seek Him and pursue His knowledge and wisdom. He expects us to pursue and the Word of God describes this clearly for us.

> *It is the glory of God to conceal a matter, But the glory of kings is to search out a matter.*
> Proverbs 25:2 (NKJV)

The verse tells us that no matter how much God tells us or shows us, there is always more to be discovered and He expects us to show initiative to discover it. Apparently God likes detective work as well. While He does leave clues and evidence, there are also things that are not readily apparent. Things that we have to look for. Without looking they will not be found. That is why Jesus said *"ask and it will be given, seek and you will find, knock and the door will be opened to you"* (Mt 7:7). Inversely Jesus was saying that if we don't ask we will not receive and if we don't seek there will be no discovery. The responsibility is ours.

It is such a noble and pure responsibility that Solomon calls it "kingship" — *"it is the glory of a king to search it out."* In today's terms kingship equals leadership and to be a leader means pursuing beyond the surface of God's communication in order to enter into the fullness of His mind. To be in a place of spiritual strength so that we are a "king" and have rulership in the spiritual realm, we have to engage in active inquiry into God's purpose. We must go beyond what is on the surface of God's communication. We have to inquire into the mind of God for greater spiritual insight and understanding.

Therefore, like a detective at a crime scene, our approach will be deductive. To deduce simply means that we will look at the evidence and ask ourselves what produced it, very much like how detectives would seek to solve a mystery. They look at the clues and fill in the gaps through deductive thinking.

Looking at the Evidence

Exhibit 1

When Moses began to confront Pharaoh on Israel's behalf in Exodus 5, the response of Israel was one of anger and rejection. They did not like Moses, they rejected his leadership and they even negotiated with Pharaoh to remain in slavery. It did not even cross their minds that they could be free. Yet, by the time the Passover came, the entire nation of Israel was heeding the commands and instructions of Moses. Every family had to kill a lamb and put blood on the doorposts of their houses lest the Angel of death kill their firstborn. In the Biblical account, not one Jewish family was afflicted by death because each father, mother and child had come to the place of hearing the voice of God through Moses and following his commands. Clearly significant transformation had taken place in the perspective and attitudes of an entire nation *before* they were delivered and we must discover what that process was like.

Exhibit 2

When Moses arrived in Egypt to confront Pharaoh, he stood as one man, with Aaron at his side, to execute God's will. But by the tenth plague the partnership was extended beyond Moses to all of Israel. An entire nation was brought into an understanding of what God was doing and acted in a manner that allowed Him to accomplish His will to set them free. At the beginning there was one man. But by the end, it was an entire nation. What facilitated this transformation that empowered all the people, not just one prophet?

Exhibit 3

At the beginning of the confrontation between God and Egypt, the picture of Israel was one of a community who fought among themselves, rejected God-ordained leadership and had no social structure except what Egypt had allowed them to have. By the time the tenth plague had arrived upon the land, Israel had become organized by families, entered into community life and care for one another, and had abandoned their own preferences to embrace God's. How did a nation become unified as the empire they lived in was becoming increasingly fragmented by successive and unrelenting crises?

Exhibit 4

When Moses first reminded the people of Israel of the promise of God to Abraham on their behalf, his words were met with disbelief and disdain. The promises of God had been relegated to mere historical accounts incapable of ever becoming relevant to their present-day reality. The people had prayed and groaned to the point that they had Heaven's attention and a deliverer was sent, but when he arrived they discounted him. They all prayed, but no one expected that deliverance would happen in their lifetime. But by the time the final plague arrived in Egypt, every Israelite was convinced that God was about to bring His word to pass and that they were the ones that was spoken of by God to Abraham hundreds of years before. Their posture had been transformed from one of disbelief to one of faith, from one of disdain to one of deep reverence. Where did this faith come from? How was it nurtured and built inside the people during a time of devastating crisis?

All of these are powerful clues that point us towards massive spiritual work being done by God in the hearts of His people, in the midst of the greatest crisis in the history of an empire. We will examine these through the following *Transformation Imperatives*:

Transformation Imperative 1: Identity is Key

Transformation Imperative 2: Faith for Fulfillment

Transformation Imperative 3: Authentic Leadership

Transformation Imperative 4: Complete Obedience

Transformation Imperative 5: Family is Everything!

Transformation Imperative 6: Community & Oneness

Transformation Imperative 7: Ultimate Partnership

Chapter 24
Transformation Imperative #1:
Identity is Key

All master-slave relationships are governed by one law —
the slave must conform to the master's concept of
who he is. The purpose of the force and brutality that
generally go along with slavery is to reinforce this law.
The first time an opinion was voiced by Moses about
Israel that was contrary to that which Ancient Egypt held,
it was met by an increase of burden, harshness and violence.

*Make the work harder for the people so that they keep
working and **pay no attention to lies.**"*

Exodus 5:9

The increase in the pressure of the life conditions (crisis) were geared towards accomplishing one thing — "let
them pay no attention to lies." What were these "lies?"
That Israel had a God of their own. That He had a purpose for them and promises made to their ancestors had to
be fulfilled in their day. And that they needed to serve and
worship Him. The issue at stake here was the exchanging
of one master for another and as a consequence one identity for another. Ancient Egypt saw this as a threat to its
very existence as an Empire. Its response was designed to
intimidate and to discourage Israel from taking the first
step towards liberation which was to embrace the opinion
of God about them. Wrong identity was the first prison of

the Israelites that God needed to smash. Without a correct identity there can be no journey forward.

Israel's enslavement to a false system is a metaphor for our enslavement in this Earth, time and the flesh until God takes us out. Until we learn to embrace and function in the fullness of our identity in Christ, we will not be able to see some of our current reflexive loyalties, desires and motivations as false. We will think we are right when in fact we are wrong. Breaking the strongholds of a wrong identity and the establishment of God's identity for us is the first step to exit. This is what Israel had to learn.

The Battle for Correct Identity

As far back as any living Israelite could remember all they knew was domination by Ancient Egypt. When Moses delivered the word of the Lord to Pharaoh, he made a startling pronouncement regarding the identity of the Israelites:

> *Then you shall say to Pharaoh, 'Thus says the LORD:* **"Israel is My son, My firstborn."**
> *Exodus 4:22 (NKJV)*

The first Transformation Imperative is the need to embrace God's identity for us. This is the core of the battle for exit. A firstborn has status. He cannot be a slave nor can he be subject to oppression. Israel's first step towards liberation was to embrace God's perspective on who they were. Even though their physical circumstances had not changed, their self-concept had to change first and be conformed to what God was declaring over their lives.

What a mindbender this must have been for Israel to hear this, let alone for Pharaoh! Both Israel and Pharaoh thought that the Israelites were slaves. After all, 400 years of history backed up this perspective. So did their poverty, lack of influence, the bruises about their bodies from frequent whippings, the hardship of their daily life and the list went on and on. They were hostage to the ruling empire of the day and they had been coded through history to accept servitude as normal life. There was no hope in the natural of escape from the circumstances that had kept them and their fathers enslaved for the last 400 years. Yet into this very real imprisoning and limiting set of circumstances thunders the voice of God — **"You are My Son, My Firstborn!"**

In declaring this to Ancient Egypt, God puts a choice before Israel. Either they continued to believe the identity Ancient Egypt had imposed upon them or they begin to believe God's opinion of

> *Correct identity disconnects us from the system which God is judging and plugs us into the life that flows to us from eternity.*

them. On the one hand, you had 400 years of evidence and on the other you had six simple words from God — "You-are-My-Son,-My-Firstborn." But those six words could change everything. To accept that they were God's firstborn son is to begin to question their position of servitude in Ancient Egypt, to develop a disdain for anything Egyptian and to reject the opinion of Ancient Egypt as false and irrelevant. It encourages internal rebellion by pointing them away from seeing Egypt as master and towards accepting God as their new master. It begins to shift loyalties and to begin to direct their life investments away from the false system of Ancient Egypt towards an eternal future with God. In other words, correct identity disconnects us from the system which God is judging and plugs us into the life that flows to us from eternity. The more this process accelerates within us, the greater the distinction made between us as believers and those who do not know the Lord.

Who Are You?

Like the children of Israel we have to come to know who God says we are and we have to reject the definitions

> *A firstborn has status, he is not a slave nor is he subject to oppression.*

pushed on us by our circumstances. As believers, the identity we are commanded by the Lord to walk in, does not come from the Earth. It is of Christ and therefore comes from the mind of God. But we are told in the scriptures that while we are not of this world, we are certainly in it. And being "in this world" means that our true identity in Christ is assailed daily by earthly influences that oppose our movement to become who God says we are. The Earth defines us based on things like our ethnicity, socio-economic background, family or national origin, career and educational achievements, and many other things. We are commanded to break the strongholds of these wrong identifiers, regardless of how powerful they may be or who agrees with them.

The Transformation Imperative of embracing God's identity is not a general requirement. It is specific, targeted and personalized. You and I, and every believer, must authoritatively reject who we used to be and embrace who God says we are. We are like Jeremiah, called by God, but weak and deficient in ourselves. God is thundering from Heaven with the declaration *"do not say I am only a child, for you must go to everyone I send you to and say whatever I command you"* (Jer 1:7). We are God's firstborn and we have to deal with our immaturity and deficiencies so we become who God says that we are.

Crisis Facilitates Identity[13]

It is impossible to separate Israel's journey to correct identity from the circumstances that surrounded them in Ancient Egypt. The crisis in Egypt played a significant part

---

[13] The content for this section is taken from Dr. Noel Woodroffe's teaching on Representation. First released within Elijah Centre in 2004 as "Ruler-ship and Representation", the teaching was later distributed to all of Congress WBN in 2011 under the heading "Representation". The saints of the Congress are very familiar with the principles of this chapter. Used by permission.

in moving their faith and belief to the place where they could follow the Lord and Moses out into the wilderness. Consider the following scripture:

> ...**On the day that I struck** all the firstborn in the land of Egypt, I sanctified to Myself all the firstborn in Israel....
>
> Numbers 3:13 (NKJV)

This verse indicates that there was a dual divine agenda behind the crisis of Ancient Egypt. The first was the destruction of the empire of Ancient Egypt. The second was the "setting apart" of a people as

> *The day of crisis is a day of identity.*

His "firstborn." One was obvious and could be seen by everyone, but the second was more important to God and it had to be spiritually discerned. As God smashes the systems of the Earth, He is setting apart an identity-filled people for Himself. The sign of our legal change of status and elevation in the spirit realm is the intensifying crises in the systems of the Earth.

Both the striking down (modern crisis) and the setting apart (God resourcing and elevating His people) happen on the same "day." The day of crisis is a day of identity. What could be seen on the Earth was the dismantling of economic, political and social life, but in the realm of the spirit a more important, powerful movement was taking place. God set apart a firstborn for Himself. It is a "bi-directional" movement occurring and both are initiated by God.

This scriptural perspective changes our view of the crises. We are not victims who cringe when economic meltdown happens or when life becomes more difficult because of the next crisis. Crisis does not intimidate us or produce fear. When I know that my identity is tied to massive global movements of crisis in the systems of the Earth, I am empowered to stand in faith and the joy of being set apart and called God's firstborn far outweighs the stress of the crises. It also produces a strong sense of responsibility — I must change and become the firstborn that God says that I am. I must align myself with His definitions and standards because much is riding on my obedience.

Embracing Our Firstborn Identity is Our Readiness for Exit

It is impossible to be the firstborn and remain a slave. The two identities are directly opposed to each other and only one can prevail. There is a link between firstborn and supremacy: *"And he is the head of the body, the church; he is the beginning and the firstborn from among the dead, so that in everything he might have the supremacy"* (Col 1:18). Christ is the Firstborn so that in everything He might have supremacy. The word "supremacy" is the Greek word *proteuo* and it means to be in the first position with the implication of high rank and prominence. He is not under devils or subject to principalities. He is over them *"Seated him at his right hand in the heavenly realms, far above all rule and authority, power and dominion, and every title that can be given, not only in the present age but also in the one to come"* (Ep 1:20,21).

> It is impossible for the firstborn to remain a slave.

To have supremacy is to live above the Darkness of the world. Whether we live in a poor nation or a rich one, a big house or small hut, we must not be dominated by the Earth or by the definitions of the Earth. Our perspective is elevated above our circumstances or situation. Therefore, neither blessing nor crisis can define us. We do not become arrogant or discouraged. As God's firstborn we have supremacy above these definitions. Being defined by God and coming into identity sets us free from the things that otherwise would define us. We have the power to reject those things because of the status God is bestowing on us as His firstborn.

Being firstborn is to be above all else just as Christ is the highest ranking and He stands above the Earth. It means to have superior status. Nothing is above it. Nothing can rule over us or master us, including Time or its many crises. Our liberation *must* translate into a desire to be with God forever. We are breaking out of our imprisonment of Time to go to our Promised Land of Eternity with Him. We are the firstborn and we have a right to be free to worship the Lord.

Embracing our identity as God's firstborn will require fundamental redefinition of many things within us. It will require that we abandon how we have been taught to know ourselves and embrace instead the Lord's identity for us. We have to become as little children in order to enter God's preferred identity for us. We have to stand on a platform of pure faith to accept whatever definition our Father describes to us. Our posture for transformation must be one of "Lord, I believe. Now help my unbelief" as He leads into a glorious identity from slaves to firstborn sons.

Chapter 25
Transformation Imperative #2:
Faith for Fulfillment

In the natural Jesus looked like any other man. He had two arms and legs and needed to sleep, eat and drink. He even had to pay taxes. We know he grew older through time because we see Him as a baby, a twelve year old and then at thirty. Time passed for Him like it did for everyone around Him. He grew up in a poor region of the country that was known for its backwardness, thus one disciple asked "can anything good come out of Nazareth?" (Jn 1:45) There was nothing in the natural to suggest that He was in fact the Son of God.

When Peter identified Jesus as "the Christ, the Son of the Living God" (Matt. 16:16), it is one of the most amazing events in the Bible. I always marvel at the courage and boldness it must have

> *We have to look beyond the natural to hear from another realm in order to look at what seems ordinary and see its extraordinariness.*

taken for Peter to have said this plainly and openly. In order for Peter to have made his declaration, he had to look past the natural to "see" that the ordinary looking man in front of him was in fact not ordinary at all. Jesus said "flesh and blood" did not reveal the truth to him but the Father in heaven. In other words, if left to the natural, we will never know what the truth of God and His purpose is.

We have to look beyond the natural to hear from another realm in order to look at what seems ordinary and see its extraordinariness. Jesus said that it is upon this "rock" that He will build His Church. The "rock" here is the ability to receive sight, discernment and understanding from Heaven in order to respond and act correctly in the midst of natural events and circumstances. It is revelation that looks past the surface of things into the truth of God. We also have to stand upon this "rock" in order to perceive the significance of the season we are living in and the required responses we must have to it.

There is Always a Time and a People

All God's prophetic promises have to come to pass. Every believer understands that whatever God says is going to be fulfilled. This means that at some point in time, the prophetic promise will come to pass in the time of a specific generation. The people who are alive at the time of its fulfillment will not be superhuman or extraordinary. They will be normal human beings just like you and me, but who happen to find themselves living in the time of prophetic fulfillment. But just like it was for Peter, it takes faith to say that it is happening now and that we are the generation.

On the Day of Pentecost it was Peter once again who stood in front of the multitude gathered and quoted the ancient prophecy of Joel and uttered the words, "this is what was spoken by the prophet Joel" (Acts 2:16). Even though Joel's words were spoken hundreds of years before, Peter recognized that he and the people of his day were living in a time of prophetic fulfillment and openly declared it to be so. Jesus Himself demonstrated this posture of readiness to take responsibility for the fulfillment of prophetic scripture when after being baptized by John, proclaimed by Heaven as the Son of God, and being tested in the wilderness, He proceeded directly to the synagogue, read from the prophecies of Isaiah and said "Today this scripture is fulfilled in your hearing" (Luke 4:21). These powerful examples give us our next Transformation Imperative — **Faith for Prophetic Fulfillment in Our Day**.

Faith Makes for Peace in Times of Crisis

Israel was taught by God to develop faith as the crisis in Ancient Egypt escalated. One of the internal shifts required for the Israelites to exit Ancient Egypt was to actually believe that God's prophetic promises were literally coming to pass

> *It takes sight, courage and faith to say "It is here. It is now. It is me."*

in their day. They had to come to a place of internal conviction that when God spoke to Abraham hundreds of years before, that He was actually talking about them. What a leap of faith! It is always easier to defer hope to some obscure future. It takes sight, courage and faith to say *"It is here. It is now. It is me."*

These same Israelites got up and went to work in the brick making factories like their forefathers had done for multiple generations over a period of 400 years. They lived in Dothan as their fathers had, probably ate about the same food and were oppressed under the same general conditions of slavery. Different Pharaohs had come and gone, but the system that enslaved them was basically the same as it had always been. They had the same last names and were organized by the 12 tribes that defined life ever since Jacob's sons had followed Joseph down to Egypt centuries before. Yet despite all of their similarities they weren't the same as those who lived before them — they were an ultimate generation, a people living at a time of fulfillment of God's promises.

Being able to recognize and embrace the time of prophetic fulfillment is very critical. Jesus lamented over

Jerusalem's failure to recognize that they were living in the days of the prophesied arrival of the Messiah and did not know it.

> *Now as He drew near, He saw the city and wept over it,*
>
> *saying, "If you had known, even you, especially in this your day, the things that make for your peace! But now they are hidden from your eyes.*
>
> *For days will come upon you when your enemies will build an embankment around you, surround you and close you in on every side,*
>
> *and level you, and your children within you, to the ground; and they will not leave in you one stone upon another, because you did not know the time of your visitation."*
>
>

Luke 19:41-44 (NKJV)

There are several significant things stated by Jesus here. The first is that he described the time as Jerusalem's Day ("your day" in v.41). He did not say "God's day." He put ownership and responsibility squarely upon the shoulders of those living in Jerusalem at that particular time. In God's mind it was Jerusalem's day and He expected them to take full possession and responsibility for it. But they did not know it. The principle here is that prophetic fulfillment does not only occur by Sovereign power. It also requires human faith, conviction and acceptance. Jesus wept because even though He was God in all His power and wanted with all His might to bring "peace" to Jerusalem, He was constrained by the fact that Jerusalem did not embrace their day and shoulder their responsibility in it.

This same pattern existed in Ancient Egypt with Israel. No matter how much God wanted to bring Israel out, if they did not believe, have faith and follow the instructions given by Moses on the Night of the Passover, no one was going to come out. Every family would have been

> *Prophetic fulfillment does not only occur by Sovereign power. It also requires human faith, conviction and response.*

struck by tragedy on that night and the entire plan of the Lord would have been dashed to pieces. But their faith and their taking of responsibility in "their day" gave the power of God the freedom to move through the land knowing that His people were safe under the cover of righteousness. What an example for us as we see God move through the systems of the global empire of our time.

Jesus said that Jerusalem did not know the things that make for their "peace." One of the meanings of the word "peace" in the original Greek is the exemption from the rage and havoc of war. The exemption is not from the war but from the devastating effects of war just as it was for Israel on the night of the Passover. The Angel of the Lord passed through the entire land. It did not make a distinction between Israel and Egypt based on genetics. Rather the distinction was made on the basis of whose house bore the marks of faith and conviction concerning the promise of the Lord for exit. Faith for prophetic fulfillment is necessary for us to walk through the crisis. Without it we will not be able to know "our day" and the things that "make for our peace."

The last thing that Jesus stated was that Jerusalem did not know the time of their "visitation." The word "visitation" in the original Greek means investigation or inspection. It refers to the act by which God looks into and searches out the ways, deeds and character of men in order to adjudge them their lot accordingly. The implications of the word are soberingly clear. To inspect or investigate implies that one is looking for something specific. God was looking for certain qualities and characteristics in Jerusalem in the day of prophetic fulfillment, and because Israel did not know it they failed to prepare themselves accordingly. As a result, God looked and He did not find.

May this never be the pronouncement of Heaven in our time. In the time of crisis, a specific kind of response, development and maturity must exist in the Earth. But the pursuit of these elements is dependent upon the faith that lives in the hearts of those whose day comes upon them.

Faith Requires Alignment Even Before Fulfillment Comes

Israel had to negotiate their way to this place. That which was hoped for, prayed for and longed for for so long was actually coming to pass in their day. They were the actual point of fulfillment of God's prophetic promises. With this revelation they had to shed any sense of their insignificance and step into a new functionality in the purposes of God. They were being required to think of themselves in a way that they never had before. They now had to step into a new level of responsibility and partnership with the Lord in the fulfillment of His purposes because it is only through willing, conscious human partnership can God's purposes come to pass. They had to begin to angle their lives in faith towards departure from Ancient Egypt even while the empire was still standing and holding them prisoner.

Note the instruction of the Lord through Moses to the people on the night of the Passover. They were instructed to eat the sacrificed lamb in the following manner:

And thus you shall eat it: with a belt on your waist, your sandals on your feet, and your staff in your hand. So you shall eat it in haste. It is the LORD's Passover.

Exodus 12:11 (NKJV)

They were required to dress for journey and departure. Bear in mind they were required to assume this posture *before* Pharaoh

> God's people had to stand in the place of faith before departure came.

134

had actually agreed to let them to leave. There was absolutely no indication in the natural that departure was coming. Nine plagues in a row had ended the same way — with Pharaoh hardening his heart and refusing to let them go. But it was an act of faith. It was a statement made to God by a generation who by their actions said: *"I know You are ready to fulfill Your word. And I believe that we are the ones through whom You will do so. The time is now and we are ready!"* What a statement of faith! God's people had to stand in this place of faith before departure came. As it was in the days of Ancient Israel so it is now with us.

It is imperative for us as it was for Israel in their day to understand what "wearing a belt on our waist, sandals on our feet and staff in our hands" means for us today? How does this translate into practical adjustments to how we build our marriages, family life and communities? What does this mean for my personal walk in Christ and my relationship to His purpose in my time? Whatever the answers are for each of us personally, they must all bring us to the same place — a lifestyle posture of faith for prophetic fulfillment in our time and of unwavering commitment to the highest levels of obedience to the word of God and partnership with His unfolding purposes.

The escalating crisis around us is not just a message to Modern America. It is more critically a clarion call to God's people to stand in faith at this time. Not faith to avoid the crisis, but faith to live through the crisis unto fulfillment of God's promise of eternity with Him. God is ready to fulfill His word in our day. All He requires is a people in the Earth to synchronize their lives with Heaven's intent just as Israel did in their day. The last plague that broke the back of the empire of Ancient Egypt took place when God's people came into complete agreement and perfect alignment with God's intent.

Chapter 26
Transformation Imperative #3
Authentic Leadership

In the heat of the current crisis God is mercifully expos-
ing deficiencies in leadership within His Church. He
wants His people to be led towards

| Leaders must go through an intense process of development. |

Him and equipped to stand in the
heat of the crisis. Those at risk
today are: a) leaders who hold a position of responsibility
but no true spiritual authority b) those who have outward
respect but have not hammered out the ways of the Lord
in their own lives that others can follow c) the many who
hold titles of authority but without the character. Leaders
must go through an intense process of development, and
once again the prophetic metaphor is useful as it reveals
Moses' growth and transformation as a man and an emerging leader. The hand of God was upon Moses from the
time he was a baby, and God crafted his life experiences and
prepared him for his life's mission of marching a people out
of an empire towards the Promised Land. There are several things that we can note about Moses' life which bears
the marks of an authentic leader.

Stripped of Nationalism

*By faith Moses, when he became of age, refused to be
called the son of Pharaoh's daughter,*

> *choosing rather to suffer affliction with the people of God*
> *than to enjoy the passing pleasures of sin.*
>
> *Hebrews 11:24,25 (NKJV)*

Moses grew up in Ancient Egypt in the house of Pharaoh as a prince. He was educated in the Egyptian system, taught all of its laws, its culture and its standards. He fully enjoyed the benefits of his princely status and was reputed to have been very intelligent, confident and outspoken as a young man. Moses was an Egyptian of Egyptians. When God took him out of Egypt however, one of the things He did was to strip Moses of any sense of loyalty to Egypt. For 40 years, Moses was banished to live in the desert and during that period he underwent such intense processing that when God was finished with him, the once outwardly impressive and eloquent Egyptian became a stammering old man. If Moses had remained embedded within his nationalistic fervor and loyalty to the system, he would not be able to do what God called him to do.

Nationalism can be a toxin to spiritual leadership because it can build a false system of loyalty which will affect a leader's ability to hear God accurately. It can create a filter that presumes the correctness of the national standard which leads to severe warps in interpreting and understanding God's purposes. Moses had to learn that God was neither Egyptian nor Israelite. His standards are above any nation and this is where authentic leadership is positioned to declare the word of the Lord. Moses' 40 years in the wilderness was designed by the Lord to wipe Egypt's influence from his mind so he could confront the system and bring God's people out.

Also stated within this process is Moses' deliverance from family norms — he refused to be called the son of Pharaoh's daughter. Empires build dynasties and pass down economic strength to their children, who become heirs based on their natural blood line — a description which too often describes modern ministries which assume the mantle must transfer to a natural successor. But true leadership rejects the authority of the family line to determine who is called by God, a lesson reinforced when Moses commissioned Joshua and not one of his natural children to lead the people after his death.

Stripped of Carnal Power

One day…Moses…saw an Egyptian beating a Hebrew, one of his own people…

…he killed the Egyptian and hid him in the sand.

The next day…he saw two Hebrews fighting. He asked the one in the wrong, "Why are you hitting your fellow Hebrew?"

The man said, "Who made you ruler and judge over us?….

Exodus 2:11-14

Moses was called to be a deliverer of the Jews, a leader who would take them out from Egyptian bondage. He seems to have had an inner desire for justice and a hatred of oppression even before he realized God's call on his life. He was certainly outraged enough that an Egyptian was beating a Hebrew that he killed the oppressor. We can see the same quest for justice when he confronted the one in the wrong in the fight between two Hebrews. But Moses used his physical strength in his first attempts to judge the people and free them from oppression and his unsuccessful efforts were obvious — the very people he was called to help rejected his authority.

The Israelite asked Moses *"who made you…?"* and this is a vital question every leader must grapple with before the Lord. When he relied on his sense of justice and his own ability to intervene, Moses failed. God had to strip Moses of his own strength because the exercise of carnal power is illegitimate in the sight of God, even when that power is used for a righteous cause.

Some leadership in today's Church is based in personal strength and carnal power. But ministries that exist in the power of a leader's gifting, energy or ability will not be able to withstand the assault of the spirit realm against the Church in a day of crisis. God frustrates everyone who tries to exercise initiative born out of human energy and personal power. His intent is to strip us of our own strength so that we rely on His power working in us. Moses was the most humble man in the entire Earth (Num 12:3). He was broken by God, shunted off to the wilderness for forty years and stripped of his power so that when he returned to deliver the people it was in the authority of the Spirit of God.

Identification with the People

By faith Moses, when he became of age, refused to be called the son of Pharaoh's daughter,

choosing rather to suffer affliction with the people of God *than to enjoy the passing pleasures of sin.*

Hebrews 11:24,25 (NKJV)

Moses was a leader of great authority. He called down plagues and confronted the most powerful political empire of his day. He had regular appointments with the emperor and had familiarity with palace life. But Moses never separated himself in his mind and heart from the people he led. He was a leader who identified very powerfully with the people even when it cost him to do so. His leadership status and position was never used to create a false distinction between himself and the people. In fact it was

> *God stripped Moses of his own strength because the exercise of carnal power is illegitimate in the sight of God, even when that power is used for a righteous cause.*

just the opposite. His leadership was validated by his identification with them.

This is an important definer. If leaders identify with the condition, challenges and process of followers then their leadership will proceed with compassion, humility and redemptive intent. The extreme use of titles and the imposition of ecclesiastical hierarchy produce separation and they disqualify one for leadership. This is the powerful example of Christ in coming to the Earth as a human being to participate in the human condition in order to redeem us back to God. This is the pattern of authentic leadership.

An Ordered Family Life

This is one of the most significant definers of authentic leadership. Moses learned this lesson early on in his development. In fact immediately after he received his dramatic call into ministry and proceeded to head off to Egypt, the Bible tells us that God "sought to kill him" (Ex 4:24). God was angry with Moses and proceeded to judge him be-

> *A man who confronted and broke the back of an empire still found the time, focus and energy to sustain a standard of marriage and family that was acceptable to God.*

cause his family had not been brought into alignment — he had not circumcised his son. God only relented when Zipporah, Moses' wife, forcibly circumcised their son. It is important to consider that God was prepared to abort the call on Moses' life and delay something as important as the liberation of millions of people because the leader's son was not circumcised. It seems a little excessive in the natural but it demonstrates the thinking system of God.

Authentic spiritual leadership must have balanced, whole and healthy family lives. Paul instructed Timothy in this when he said that *"If a man does not know how to rule his own house, how will he take care of the church of God"* (1 Tim 3:5)? There are many ministries which have been aborted because of deficient marriages and family lives. The ministry tends to take precedent over the maintenance of this core structure of a leader's life.

> *Becoming a servant produces deliverance from the inherent corruption that comes by access to privilege, power and material things.*

God ensured that Moses understood the danger of this, and clearly he learned his lesson because God never tried to kill him again. The implication here is that a man who confronted and broke the back of an empire still found the time, focus and energy to sustain a standard of marriage and family that was acceptable in the sight of God.

Effective Stewardship

As a prince of Egypt Moses had legitimate right to everything in the land. But when God stripped him of his wealth and position he made him instead one who took care of another man's sheep. A steward is different from an owner. Though the steward has great authority he always has at the back of his mind that all that he has been given power over does not belong to him. It is in taking care of another man's sheep that Moses began to develop his sense of accountability, transparency and loyalty. He learned the value of servant-hood and humility and it was from that position that he exercised massive authority when he called down plagues on Ancient Egypt.

The people that we lead are not "ours" and regardless of our spiritual stature and history we have no right to claim ownership of that which is the Lord's. We are stewards of God's purpose and of His people. Our responsibility is to point the people to the Lord through accurate demonstration of the ways of the Lord which have been built within our own lives. Effective stewardship inoculates against pride. A true servant humbly seeks his master's will. Becoming a servant produces deliverance from the inherent corruption that comes by access to privilege, power and material things. Authentic leaders demonstrate the values of restraint, diligence and humility in the execution of their responsibilities. Where these elements are missing, authentic spiritual leadership is not present.

Dealing with Deficient Leadership

Many believers have been damaged by deficient leadership. While every situation is unique, there are many ways leaders hurt or sabotage followers. Some blatantly sin and thereby break the spiritual momentum necessary to build spiritually. And many who do sin do not repent properly, dooming the ministry to years of agonizing brokenness. Other leaders want only to build their own empire and they relate to people out of a mercenary motivation. People leave feeling taken advantage of and used up. Perhaps the most often played out scenario is where God-ordained leaders simply fail to keep growing themselves. They stagnate because they stop going to God and becoming more spiritually substantial in order to meet the challenges of a new season. They begin in the zeal of the authentic call of God and they prepare themselves. But at some point they plateau spiritually and while they may be good and decent people, they lose the ability to lead followers into the next place in God. Their works have replaced relationship with God.

How must we respond to deficient leadership? Many people become cynical assuming that authentic leaders do not exist. Others come to see strength as oppressive. This causes many to reject authority and de-emphasize the importance of leadership by putting emphasis almost exclusively on body ministry or some other type of forum that allows for a loose association without requirements from appointed leadership. But as we see in the case of Israel, without Moses there would have been no deliverance.

Paul said that the people should *"follow me as I follow Christ"* (1 Cor 11:1), revealing two dynamics. The first is that leaders are required. The Church is not a society of people of equal rank. Paul did not say "I'm following Christ, you follow Him too." He said "follow me." He wasn't being arrogant or building a cult following. These scriptures teach us that leadership is essential and part of God's design for His Kingdom. But there is a second dynamic. Leaders must be legitimate and authentic, filled with Christ-likeness for it is only as Paul followed Christ that he could lead people towards God. Implicit in Paul's statement is that if a leader stops following Christ we are authorized to reject their leadership. Therefore we have to know Christ for ourselves so we are not deceived into following that which is incorrect.

In this chapter we have looked at five characteristics of authentic leadership in Moses' life: a) stripped of nationalism b) stripped of carnal power c) identification with the people d) ordered family life e) effective stewardship. Growth indicates a process of development over time and these characteristics can be useful for leaders who can consider this Biblical account as a grid to place over their lives to measure their own growth into authentic leadership. Followers can also utilize it to examine existing leadership systems to ensure accuracy.

Chapter 27
Transformation Imperative #4
Complete Obedience

On a recent flight from Miami into the UK we experienced a good bit of turbulence. The pilot made several altitude changes and lateral diversions as we streaked across the Atlantic at 37,000 feet. It was fine because we were generally heading northward. But the closer we got to London the more precise our flight path became. The aircraft cannot land "approximately" at an airport or city. It must touch down at the exact spot of designated arrival. Miles away from the airport, the plane was bounced all over the sky. But at the point of approach to the airport, the pilot has no more leeway. The tower directs the aircraft with specific instructions that have to be obeyed. There is no flying around storms or changing altitudes. There is only a precise point of touchdown which must be hit regardless of the prevailing conditions.

This metaphor is useful as we consider approaching the final destination of immortality. We use it quite a bit in Congress WBN to relay two key realities. The first is that the Finish is the point of ultimate accuracy. Just as a plane enters a zone in which it must obey every command from the tower, we have to bring our lives into complete obedience to the Lord in order to reach the ultimate destination. The second indicates that regardless of crises, as we approach immortality we have to "fly through them" and move unswervingly towards the Finish. Putting the two together: *accuracy in the midst of crisis is the requirement for the Church of the End Times.*

That is what happened to the Israelites in Ancient Egypt. Crisis after crisis assaulted Ancient Egypt as they approached their exit, but they never diverted. Their obedience reached a climax when the Angel of death swept through the nation. The people of God stayed in their homes and obeyed specific instructions given by God: to take a lamb, including what kind of lamb it had to be, how to cook it, how to apply the blood on their doors, what to wear when they ate, etc. Over and over the people are told to *"obey these instructions"* (v 24), and their response is recorded:

✔ *The Israelites did just what the LORD commanded Moses and Aaron (v 28)*

✔ *The Israelites did as Moses instructed (v 35)*

✔ *All the Israelites did just what the LORD had commanded Moses and Aaron (v 50)*

Their absolute belief in the voice of God was expressed through complete obedience to His commands. The whole nation became prophetic as they heard and obeyed the Lord's commands through Moses, commands that guided them through the crisis to a point of safety and ultimate deliverance. The more

> **The Prophetic**
> The prophetic is not just a gift or a ministry in the Church, it is a lifestyle embraced by every believer who hears and obeys the voice of God in everyday life.
>
> All of God's people becoming prophetic cannot be limited to individual prophecies given over each other. This is a valid and Biblical practice, but the prophetic goes far beyond it.
>
> The prophetic is an operating system for life, or we could say the voice of God is the substructure of every aspect of my life.
>
> We have written extensively about the prophetic in other books you can find on our websites.

powerful the crisis, the more exact the obedience required and so it is with us. God will guide us and preserve us during the depths of the crisis, providing specific instructions that we must obey.

The key to our successful arrival at God's intended destination is the voice of God. We must become prophetic and walk in complete obedience to His commands. There are three things we see in Israel's process which produced within them powerful and complete obedience: a) abandon self-based lifestyle and preferences b) knowledge and awareness must be made the possession of all c) trust in God appointed leadership.

Abandon Self-Based Lifestyles and Preferences

Israel had to reject any internal position which considered their personal agenda, desires or preferences as primary. They had to develop a mentality where the preferences of God took precedence over their own. The will and commands of God became their only anchor and hope in the crisis. For example, specific and clear prophetic commands were given about how to eat on the night God delivered them (Ex 12). They were to kill a lamb at dusk and it had to be roasted over a fire, not eaten raw or boiled; the entire lamb had to be eaten or what was left destroyed in the fire. They had to eat it inside the house while they were dressed for immediate departure. Even their children had to be awake and eating, ready to travel late in the night. Blood had to be applied to their doorposts while they sat inside the house. No one could go outside.

Imagine if people had imposed their personal preferences. One man wants boiled lamb while another preferred to feed his family on the patio rather than inside the house. Another feels the children are too tired and should be allowed to sleep. Another just remodeled his house and doesn't want to put blood on the freshly painted door. These desires or preferences in and of themselves are not bad or evil, but if Israel related to God out of their own preferences the Angel of death would have struck their homes. He was sent after all those who did not have this Divinely prescribed order within their house. It was not a time for personal preferences and opinions about what should be done. It was a day of complete obedience.

In a time of crisis we need to hear from heaven and obey precisely what God commands us. The children of Israel were told to *"Obey these instructions"* and in fact *"The Israelites did just what the Lord commanded Moses and Aaron"* (Ex 12:24,28). The children of Israel walked in complete obedience. Heeding the instructions of the Lord — being prophetic in not just hearing but also obeying — was vital and was the beginning of their capacity for complete obedience. Any doctrine or ministry that promotes the pursuit of self-generated life preferences is in fact condemning God's people to certain destruction.

Knowledge and Awareness Must Be Made the Possession of All

What is clear in the account of Israel's preparation for the Night of the Passover was the fact that everyone was aware of what God was doing. His move-

> *Knowledge and awareness enable complete obedience.*

ments were no longer the preserve of Moses' knowledge alone. They had been made the possession of the entire nation through Moses' leadership and commands. This clearly was important to God. Even after Israel left Egypt and were making their way across the wilderness, the structure of their journey included not only God's instructions to Moses, but also His presence in the form of pillars of cloud and fire in plain view of all the people.

Therefore, not only were knowledge and awareness requirements for surviving the tenth plague, but God later made it a fundamental structure of their journey to the Promised Land. Everyone could see the Presence of God and the direction in which He was heading even as they submitted to Moses as their leader.

Knowledge and awareness enable complete obedience. Complete obedience is more than just blindly following instructions. It is followership that is informed about what they are doing and why it needs to be done. There must be understanding behind the compliance in order for it to be complete obedience. Consider the words of Jesus when He expressed to His disciples His desire to fully disclose to them everything He knew:

> *No longer do I call you servants, for a servant does not know what his master is doing; but have called you friends, for **all things that I heard from My Father I have made known to** you.*
>
> *John 15:15 (NKJV)*

A servant can comply and still not understand his master's intent. But a friend offers compliance with understanding because he has been empowered through the knowledge of "all things." This is the desire of God for His Body. This expression of desire by Christ carries implications for both leaders and followers. For leaders, there is the requirement to diligently and consciously empower people through effective distribution of the resource God has given for the people. For followers there is the requirement to consciously pursue knowledge and awareness of what God is doing. His desire is to make it known to those who seek.

The journey of the children of Israel from slavery into freedom and possession of their Promised Land is a description of becoming prophetic. Moses declared that he wished that all of God's people were prophets and the

Lord would put His spirit on them (Num 11:29), and on the Night of the Passover every single house heard and obeyed the command of the Lord through Moses. Moses' heart was always for complete distribution of God's speaking to the entire nation. The Lord gave the law to Moses but he made it the possession of the people (Heb 9:19). Moses was known as the friend of God (Exodus 33:11). It is into this friendship he sought to bring Israel when he stated that he wished that all the Lord's people were prophets. Moses understood the heart of God and he knew that if knowledge and awareness were made a part of the people, then partnership and complete obedience would be secured.

Trust in God-appointed Leadership

There would have been no exit without Moses and Moses would not have been successful in his mission if the people did not grow to trust him and follow the

> *Trust cannot be demanded, it must be earned through consistent lifestyle and sustained accuracy of leadership.*

commands he relayed to them from the Lord. God was moving in Ancient Egypt and He used Moses as His spokesman. The people had to come to recognize that Moses heard from God and was a trustworthy leader. Trust cannot be demanded. It must be earned through consistent lifestyle and sustained accuracy of leadership. In this regard, the journey through ten plagues was not merely about devastating the empire but more critically about bringing Israel to the place where they could trust Moses' leadership, which was affirmed again and again by the Lord.

Later as they journeyed across the wilderness God allowed all the people to see the pillar of cloud by day and fire by night, and they all could see when it moved. Yet Moses still commanded the people that it was time to migrate and move with the cloud which they themselves could plainly see: *"At the LORD's command they encamped, and at the LORD's command they set out. They obeyed the LORD's order, in accordance with his command through Moses"* (Num 9:23). God moved and everyone in the nation could plainly see the cloud moving, but God still required Moses to command the people that it was time to migrate. This is perfected society created by God — He is commanding His people and the leaders He has called and appointed must be in absolute agreement and alignment with Him and therefore worthy to be followed.

We are aware that the numerous occurrences of moral and ethical failings of leaders within the church world have had the effect of creating cynicism, fear and withholding in the hearts of many believers. But God will not change the system He set in place for our spiritual journey. That system is God's leadership must be faithfully represented by humans to other humans. It is not the system that has failed, but it is the humans who have failed the system. The children of Israel themselves had to work through all the negative mental impact of oppressive leadership imposed on them through 400 years of slavery. Everything in their memory indicated that leaders were oppressive, wicked and self-centered. But God began to speak and an internal reformation had to occur — a change that empowered them to see Godly leadership as essential to exit and journey towards their inheritance.

When we place our trust in God-ordained leadership, the Lord will deal with those He has placed in a position of authority. When Moses misrepresented the Lord by striking the rock rather than speaking to it, God revoked his privilege to bring the nation into the Promised Land (Num 20:12). God is identifying disobedience in the Body of Christ and moving against leaders who have compromised. He wants to make sure His people are led correctly and fully into their promised inheritance. The arising and identification of stable, trustworthy leadership will heal and restore the capacity of the Body of Christ to follow faithful leaders who are themselves following Christ.

We have identified three issues in this chapter that empowered the Israelites to full and complete obedience: a) abandon self-based lifestyle and preferences b) knowledge and awareness must be made the possession of all c) trust in God appointed leadership. As we embrace them, God will instruct us and guide us through the crisis to the exact point of arrival.

Chapter 28
Transformation Imperative #5
Family is Everything!

Within Congress WBN, one of the critical areas of spiritual building has been imparting to our men the capacity for spiritual headship over their families. Over the years, we have engaged and interacted with thousands of men from different nations, cultures, tribes and languages. In each case, the urgency and priority for men to build their families was evident. Without it there can be no success in God. In helping to build this important area of our global community, we have come to realize that men are the same everywhere and at their core they carry the same concerns and confront very similar challenges.

One of the things we see in the story of Biblical Israel's Exodus is the importance that spiritual headship played in the process. It began with Moses when, after receiving in spectacular fashion the call of God to liberate His people, God sought to kill him because Moses had not circumcised his son (Ex.4:24-26). It was Moses' first lesson in what it means to say "yes" to the Lord. As we mentioned previously, God was prepared to delay His purpose to liberate millions of people in slavery because the chosen leader had one, single uncircumcised child. This shows the weight of importance God put on the issue of proper spiritual headship and family. God required that Moses become a better husband and father before he could become the mighty deliverer of a nation.

But perhaps the most significant demonstration of this emphasis in the heart of God took place during the tenth plague. The first nine plagues were worked by the hand of Moses. He received commands from the Lord and he executed them faithfully, hammering the empire of Ancient Egypt. The method of the tenth plague however was fundamentally different. Unlike previous plagues, the Lord told Moses to instruct every household:

> *Speak to all the congregation of Israel, saying: 'On the tenth of this month **every man shall take** for himself a lamb, according to the house of his father, **a lamb for a household.***

> *Then Moses called for all the elders of Israel and said to them, "**Pick out and take lambs for yourselves according to your families**, and kill the Passover lamb.*

> *And you shall take a bunch of hyssop, dip it in the blood that is in the basin, and strike the lintel and the two doorposts with the blood that is in the basin. **And none of you shall go out of the door of his house until morning.***
> Exodus 12:3,21,22 (NKJV)

The nation was mobilized for exit by families, the core unit upon which God builds a society. And in each family the man was required to rise up to a place of leadership and obedience. It was the activation of spiritual headship in the home that was at the core of Israel's deliverance. If the men failed to prepare their households, the very Angel of death would have destroyed their families and aborted God's purposes. The critical nature of activated spiritual manhood is very clear here.

The instruction of Moses to the elders of Israel ended with *"none of you shall go out of the door of his house until morning."*

At the height of the crisis, the place for men to be was standing inside their homes, leading their families through the crisis until the purpose of the Lord was secured. Without this Transformation Imperative of Renewed Emphasis on Family and Spiritual Headship, there can be no safe passage through the crisis-ridden environment of the last days.

The Attack on Spiritual Manhood

The war for the family — and for the activation of spiritual manhood — was waged against God's people long before the night of departure. The move to abort and kill all male children was given by Pharaoh years before, a genocide incited by the dark spiritual powers behind Ancient Egypt.

> *At the height of the crisis, the place for men to be was standing in their homes, leading their families until the purpose of the Lord was secured.*

> *And [the king of Egypt] said, "When you do the duties of a midwife for the Hebrew women, and see them on the birthstools, if it is a son, then you shall kill him; but if it is a daughter, then she shall live."*
>
> *Exodus 1:16 (NKJV)*

The emasculation of Israel was part of the strategy by the enemy to keep them enslaved. The thinking was if there were no men, then revolt would not be possible. The midwives did not obey the command of the king and instead saved the male children. Unknowingly what they actually did was preserve the lives of those who would become the future warriors and priests unto God who would lead Israel out of slavery and into the Promised Land. Among these were the Joshuas and Calebs, the ones through whom God's purposes were to be finalized. The attack on men in Ancient Egypt was not merely against the present family structures but also the future purposes of the Lord. Spiritual manhood is critically important.

Although it is in different forms, the attack on manhood continues in our day. In some cases it is blatant and frontal, such as the horrific rise of internet pornography or the warped concepts of masculinity passed down through our culture. The increasing widespread acceptance of same sex marriage seeks to completely alter and blur basic definitions of Biblical manhood. In other ways, more subtle attacks occur, such as the standard family sitcom formula which features a competent and intelligent wife who has to bear with the antics of her buffoon husband. In all of these cases darkness targets manhood — the attack is against correct identity, placement and functionality of men in the purposes of the Lord.

This spiritual strategy affects the quality of family life. Marriages are the first to suffer. Within the Church the divorce rate is as high as out in the world (and this does not even take into consideration the number of failed marriages that do not decide to get divorced for one reason or another). With the breakdown of the marriage comes the deterioration of family life and the spiritual destruction of children as the future of what the Lord wants to do. They are cut adrift spiritually and left at the mercy of influences that steer them away from the path of the Lord. Spiritual leadership at the head has broken down and therefore the defenses around the family are shattered, leaving children open to attack. The implications of this reality for wider society should be obvious to us all. The family is the building block of the society and as it deteriorates, society as a whole suffers. It is a cascading process that can only be fixed by beginning with fundamental change at the head.

The Bible teaches us that the man is the head of the home (1 Cor. 11:3). This does not make man qualitatively better than woman. After all, the Father outranks the Holy Spirit in the Godhead, but it would be wrong to state that He is qualitatively better than the Holy Spirit. They are in fact one. It is merely a matter of spiritual ranking and responsibility. Neither does headship mean that the husband owns his wife. That is an ungodly concept that was held widely in previous times and did great damage. It simply means that he will be held ultimately responsible by God for the condition of his home. Where there is a man in the context of a marriage and family, he must shoulder his ultimate responsibility for the spiritual well being of the home *(see Sidebar)*.

The principle of headship is important because the spiritual state of the head determines the spiritual state of those under him. Therefore, if the head of the home is spiritually deactivated, then the family is left vulnerable. If the enemy can keep spiritual headship weak, then he knows that mobilization around the purposes of the Lord would not be possible.

The evidence of this strategy exists all around us. Countless ministries have been undone because of broken marital covenants and dysfunctional family lives. In most church communities, men are the group numbered among the least spiritually activated while the women tend to carry the greater weight in spiritual function. Even the message of the Church has not been able to attract men to Christ in any meaningful and significant way. With-

> **What About Women?**
>
> *Note: The issue of headship does not deny the critical role women have to play in the home and leadership of the family. Paul in his encouragement of younger widows to marry, commands them to "manage their homes" (1 Tim. 5:14).*
>
> *In the Greek, the word translates "to rule the house" and is used in Matt 21:33 to describe a master of a house. The implication here is that wives are partners in the rulership of the home with husbands even though he is the one who stands in the place of ultimate accountability.*
>
> *In the case where there is no husband, single mothers are empowered by God to provide this very important function of ruling and managing their homes before the Lord just as Paul indicated.*

out realizing it, we have been under attack and what has been compromised is the capacity of the Church to move forward in patriarchal strength. This has to be addressed by God as it was in the days of Ancient Egypt.

Rebuilding the Core of a Nation

The picture we have of Israel at the beginning of Exodus is one of a broken society without any coherent social structure or leaders of the nation. Piece by piece God started to rebuild Israel. He first gave them leaders (Moses and Aaron) and validated that leadership powerfully in the sight of all. He re-established the faith of the people in God-ordained leadership. But this was a stepping stone to a greater corporate purpose. He then used this platform of faith to get the people to hear and obey. And His first command to them concerned the mobilization of the entire nation through households. He commanded the men and pointed them back to their families. He told them *"every man shall take for himself a lamb, **according to the house of his father**, a lamb for a household"* (Ex 12:3). Suddenly a broken society now had to find out who belonged to the house of his father. They had to clarify their relationships and trace their lineage. The process deepened their sense of family identity and rebuilt their sense of history. And the men were to lead this reconstructive process.

Before they left Egypt the men were being made into the bedrock of Israel's future civilization. The journey to the Promised Land was organized around tribes and families. The people knew how to encamp around the Tabernacle by identifying their tribes and families.

> *Before they left Egypt the men were being made into the bedrock of Israel's future civilization.*

God led the nation by giving clear commands to Moses, who then relayed the word of the Lord to the elders who in turn commanded the heads of households. Finally each man commanded his family. God started to bring a broken nation into divine order and the men were crucial to this process. This responsibility to help one's family to find their accurate place in the structure of God's purposes and to deliver to them the word of the Lord should inflame the heart of every man in the Kingdom. It is our highest call and most sacred responsibility.

Our organization, Congress WBN, has been given a clear mission from the Lord to resource the Body of Christ. It is a mission that we take very seriously and which we have been pursuing for the past 23 years. God gave our men a clear and urgent emphasis from His word which has become fundamental to our advance. It is taken from a very well-known scripture:

> *(for if a man does not know how to rule **his own house**, how will he take care of the **church of God**?)*
>
> *1 Timothy 3:5 (NKJV)*

God gave the men of our world new eyes with which to view a very familiar scripture. In the past we saw this verse primarily targeting church leaders, who were required to have an orderly household and it does apply in that context. But God connected for us the rulership of every home with our global mandate to take care of and minister to His Church. God taught the men of our world to connect how they love their wives, raise their children and manage their homes to the vast, corporate mission of our Congress to take care of the Body of Christ. It did not matter that you never traveled or preached. The private life of every man was now connected to our public mission. The personal was now connected to the corporate. And with these connections every man was brought into the realm of spiritual ministry and responsibility for securing the purposes of the Lord by spiritually leading their homes.

We call our men Hebronites. It is a name taken from a family of the Tribe of Levites who had the specific responsibility of taking care of the sacred items located within the Holy of Holies of the Tabernacle of God (Num. 3:27-31). They were the only ones God allowed to transport the Ark of the Tabernacle. When the pillar of cloud or fire began to move across the wilderness, they were the ones to pack up all of God's precious and sacred items and follow after Him. They belonged to Him. They lived to serve Him. They followed God intently. And they lived to show others the path He was walking. For us, the items inside the Holy of Holies are our families and marriages. They are the core of God's world and we see ourselves as the faithful defenders of its sanctity and order.[14]

What God did with Israel during the final plague was to teach them that the core of His nation and its advance is the family and the primary covenants that secure them in place. They provide God with stability and a foundation upon which His purposes can go forward and prosper. The community life of Israel was built around the Tabernacle and the Holy of Holies which the Hebronites secured at the center of it all. If the center cannot hold, everything falls apart. It is the responsibility of headship to provide God's world with this stability and safety by keeping its core sacred and whole.

There have been far too many times throughout the history of the Church when men have allowed the purposes of God to fall to the ground because their families and marriages were not held sacred. Too many times the enemy has been able to boast over the inconsistency of men and the negative consequences of God's purposes being delayed or aborted. But that is changing. Just as God

---

[14]For more resources and information on the "Hebronites," feel free to visit www.quarrylife.com where we have documented the spiritual journey of our men and the current spiritual emphases for our manhood development.

called for men to take their place at the height of the crisis in Ancient Egypt, He is summoning men today to take their place. Men across the Earth are standing up and leading their homes into the purposes of the Lord. It is time for authentic spiritual manhood to arise as God moves to rebuild the core of the Body of Christ and prepare us for immortality.

Chapter 29
Transformation Imperative #6
Community and Oneness

The state of fracture in the Church is so intense that almost everyone has experienced the breakage of oneness and lapse of community on one level or another. The list of causes is endless: doctrinal differences, bad leadership, personal offense or relational conflict, a church refusing to move forward in the things of God or alternately actually moving forward and some people not liking the change of direction. The list goes on and on.

We have two windows through which to view the deficient quality of community life among the Hebrews in Ancient Egypt. Both reveal that dysfunction, jealousy and strife were the norm. The first portal is the life of Joseph and his brothers where it was their jealousy, hatred and betrayal that were used by the Lord to get Joseph down to Egypt in the first place. Decades passed and God's purpose came to pass. Joseph forgave his brothers and fed them and he had them brought down to live with him in the land of plenty where he treated them with kindness. They lived together in Dothan and experienced favor in Ancient Egypt, and as time passed and their father Jacob died the brothers did not hesitate to manipulate Joseph (Gen 49:15). They lied to Joseph about what their father said, decades after reconciliation and after they had all seen God's purposes fulfilled. Even then the brothers were dominated by guilt, fear and deception in their relationship with Joseph.

The next occurrence involves two Hebrews fighting and Moses seeking to intervene by asking *"Men, you are brothers; why do you want to hurt each other"* (Ex 2:13 & Acts 7:26)*?* The word used to describe their relationship is the Greek word *adelphos* and it means a brother or close kinsman. It describes people who belong to the same close-knit community based on identity and common origin, as well as persons united by a common calling and place in life. Both men were Hebrews. Both suffered under oppressive conditions. But instead of solidarity and strong community these brothers were in a violent conflict that they refused to allow Moses to mediate.

Whether it is in the golden era of Israel's favor with Joseph and his brothers, or 400 years later when they suffered under the savage oppression of slavery, the experience of the Hebrews was the same: jealousy, anger, fear, competition and deception. Deficient community life defined the nation from their origin as Jacob's dysfunctional sons all the way down to their enslavement four centuries later, but something happened when Moses was sent by God to deliver them. When the prophet returned in the strength of the Lord, one of the key tasks was the establishment of community and oneness.

> *When Moses returned in the strength of the Lord one of the key tasks was the establishment of community and oneness.*

The Whole Assembly Shall Kill "It"

Speak to all the congregation of Israel, saying: 'On the tenth day of this month every man shall take for himself a lamb, according to the house of his father, a lamb for a household.

And if the household is too small for the lamb, let him and his neighbor next to his house take it according to the number of the persons; according to each man's need you shall make your count for the lamb.

Your lamb shall be without blemish, a male of the first year. You may take it from the sheep or from the goats.

Now you shall keep it until the fourteenth day of the same month. **Then the whole assembly of the congregation of Israel shall kill it at twilight.**

Exodus 12:3-6 (NKJV)

On the Night of the Passover God ensured that His people were functioning in a place of community and oneness. As the ten plagues were released upon society,

> *The same crisis which took Egypt apart made the people of God one cohesive nation.*

they had acquired such a capacity for community life that one family's abundance could now fill up another family's lack. They learned selflessness and the value of sacrifice. They gained a new value and respect for their neighbor and brother which brought them into more committed relationship and shared identity. They had become synchronized by their common placement within the unfolding of God's purposes. The people saw God and became one.

There were 600,000 men in Israel, plus their wives and children. Some households shared a lamb, let's estimate that one third of the houses did so, which means between 300,000 – 400,000 individual animals were butchered and offered, but God describes this activity as killing "it." The sacrifice of multitudes was a singular offering in the eyes of God. What a beautiful picture! As Ancient Egypt was falling apart and fragmenting through their resistance to the word of the Lord, Israel was being reconstituted by God into wholeness, oneness and community. The same crisis which took Egypt apart, made the people of God one. This could only be the work of a sovereign God.

What the children of Israel could not have known at that time was that the there was one lamb who had been slain from the foundation of the world for all of our sins (Rev 13:8). If they hadn't come to the place of intensified joining and correct alignment with one another so that God saw not one lamb but many, it would have contradicted His eternal plan for salvation.

What Produces Community?

As we look at the nation of Israel we also want to look at ourselves to see how God wants to bring authentic oneness and community in the global Church in our day. Clearly the Oneness that God sees from the Spirit realm, and which causes Him to say thousands of lambs equal one sacrifice, cannot be built on natural mechanisms or organizational coherence. The Body of Christ is too vast and diverse to be made one organizationally. There is something beyond physical proximity in prayer meetings and gatherings that is required. The Israelites offered one sacrifice to the Lord because they had all committed themselves to the same standards and had agreed upon a common set of spiritual perspectives on life around them. Like our ancient brothers, our oneness is achieved through our common adherence to eternal principles represented in Israel as a) complete Christ-likeness b) recognizing we are aliens.

A) Complete Christ-likeness

Tell the whole community of Israel that on the tenth day of this month each man is to take a lamb for his family, one for each household.

That same night they are to eat the meat roasted over the fire…head, legs and internal organs.

Do not leave any of it till morning; if some is left till morning, you must burn it.

Exodus 12:3,8-10

The instructions were to eat the entire lamb. The application for us is clear: we must consume all of Christ-likeness within our individual lives and our families. We cannot be partially Christ-like in a day of crisis.

The fullness of Christ is described in the New Testament very clearly — it is the full operational power of all five dimensions of Christ within the Church. The gifts of Christ are apostle, prophet, evangelist, pastor and teacher and for too long these have been seen as ministries rather than what they actually are — the nature and character of Christ Himself. Each one is responsible to be an accurate receiver of that particular dimension of Christ and impart it to the wider Body of Christ to make us equipped and mature. The goal of the five is to build us up until we reach maturity and the unity of the faith and we all attain the whole measure of the fullness of Christ (Ep 4:12,13). Our brothers in Ancient Egypt ate every part of the lamb. There was complete and total consumption.

We could never be one if we start with our individual human personalities or the uniqueness of our culture. The only thing that creates true Oneness is our common possession of maturity before the Lord. It is Christ's character and ways in each of us that make us one. The single

> *The only thing that creates true Oneness is our common possession of maturity before the Lord.*

definition of Christ fits every human personality and culture, so that in our diversity we are unified and made whole. All of us started out in different places, with limited understandings of Christ and of His Kingdom. But if we are all journeying toward the fullness of Christ, we are walking more and more towards community and oneness that is only found "in Christ."

This has been something we have experienced across the vast reaches of Congress WBN. We work in 95 nations which in the natural are separated not only by geographic distance but also by culture, language, ethnicity, worldview, etc. Our common possession of apostolic grace has brought us into a great sense of oneness, a reality that was massively enhanced when in 2011 we released a series of teachings entitled Tracking Final Maturity (TFM) to all of our churches. It had an immense impact on all the people, some who sat in Fiji and others in Switzerland; in Congo and in the United States; all of them came to new levels of maturity in Christ. If you ask anyone from across our global order they could talk very coherently about their personal development process and their journey towards maturity.

Our experience reinforced the Biblical reality that the standards for Christ-likeness are universal and are universally attainable by all who desire to grow and who commit themselves to a process of development. It is possible to come to maturity and to actually grow up in Christ, and ordinary people from every walk of life are a testament to that. The spiritual resource given to valid apostles and other five-fold ministries does equip God's people; relational proximity does allow for an impartation to occur. Coming into maturity has made our tens of thousands of people more "one" before the Lord as Christ defines us more than the uniqueness of our various cultures or even our individual personality traits.

B) Recognizing we are Aliens

And thus you shall eat it: with a belt on your waist, your sandals on your feet, and your staff in your hand. So you shall eat it in haste. It is the LORD's Passover.

Exodus 12:11 (NKJV)

This is how people dressed in that time when they were going out on a long journey. It was a symbolic act by a people in the Earth indicating to Heaven that they were now ready to embark on a journey forward with God. A

> *A critical pillar upon which our oneness is built is a universal recognition that we don't belong here.*

critical pillar upon which our oneness is built is a universal recognition that we do not belong here. The darkened Earth and the realm of mortality are not "home" for us. God has set eternity in our hearts and we are looking and groaning for immortality.

Abraham is described as a stranger in a foreign country even when he lived in the Promised Land God had ordained his descendents to occupy. He lived in tents and refused to build a house because nothing on this Earth could capture his heart. He was looking forward to the city whose architect and builder is God (Heb 11:9,10). When we see God we recognize that He is our Father and we long for home to the point that *"I am a stranger to my brothers, an alien to my own mother's sons"* (Ps 69:8).

Moses named his son Gershom because the Lord had removed him from Ancient Egypt and in considering this he realized *"I have become an alien in a foreign land"* (Ex 2:22). The name Gershom means a refugee or one who has been driven away and thrust out. Moses was not declaring that he had left Ancient Egypt only, but that his homeland was not of this Earth. When he stood before Pharaoh he did so not as a citizen or ambassador of a natural nation. Pharaoh could not figure out why this man would not be reasonable nor could he understand the demand to let the people go so that they could freely worship the Lord. This was a clash of Kingdoms, one earthly and the other heavenly. If we are going to be dressed and ready for exit, we have to recognize that nothing on this Earth defines us. We must reject the definitions imposed on us by our nation, culture and even our families because we are aliens and we are ready to go "home!"

It is no accident that these two core aspects that define our community and oneness — complete Christ-likeness and recognizing that we are aliens — have been misunderstood and are the subject of intense theological debate, rendering them ineffective in the lives of believers. Regarding eschatology, there are so many differing views, each one contradicting the other to the point that the coming of the Lord divides the very Church He is coming for. We must move towards the simplicity of our brothers who sat in their homes with powerful expectation. The night of deliverance was not a remote theory or theological concept. It was an expectation that was fulfilled by the reality of God's movements. We must have an expectant mentality, dressed and ready. It is living in this state of spiritual anticipation that makes us one before the Lord.

The total consumption and appropriation of Christ-likeness has also been deeply assaulted by two equally incorrect mentalities about all five ministry gifts. The first school of thought rejects the relevance of apostles and prophets, thus eliminating essential spiritual resources required for our full maturity. The second embraces all five gifts of Christ, but incorrectly exalts them as individual ministries, putting the emphasis too much on man rather than the quantum of Christ each is meant to impart and distribute. Either error results in the wider Body of Christ not receiving the totality of Christ and not growing into full maturity.

But it is a new day of God's speaking and resourcing of His people. As God assaults the Earth with crisis, He is leading us towards true Community and Oneness just as He did with our ancient brothers. We are coming into closer unification as each of us moves towards complete maturity and Christ-likeness and together we prepare to exit this Earth in which we are aliens. We want to go home!

Chapter 30
Transformation Imperative #7:
Ultimate Partnership

There is one reason God liberated the Israelites and took them towards the Promised Land — He wanted to express His partnership with a people in the Earth. God told the Israelites they were to cross over Jordan and dispossess nations greater than themselves. This process would require a partnership in which *"He will destroy them and bring them down before you; so you shall drive them out and destroy them quickly"* (Deut 9:3). God destroyed them and Israel drove them out. This is the perfect partnership between God and His people which the Israelites had to prepare themselves for long before they reached the Jordan.

The picture of Israel is of a nation doing their part in order to exit slavery and come into their inheritance. It is a picture of man moving in sync with God to secure His purposes. It is a picture of a nation conscious of the fact that God was on the move inside the crisis. It is a picture of ultimate maturity expressing itself in perfect partnership between God and man to smash an empire and set God's people free. Let us identify a few of the patterns of Israel's partnership with the Lord inside the last plague at the height of the crisis.

Understanding Replaces Ignorance

God speaks very clearly to Israel in the crisis and in so doing removes their ignorance concerning what He was doing. In Exodus 11, God gives Moses insight into the sequence of events for the final plague. In Exodus 12 He extends this understanding to the entire nation. He brings them out of the darkness of ignorance concerning the events taking place around them. In doing so he empowers all of Israel to align their lives and responses with the intent of the Lord.

One of the foundations of the spiritual journey of Congress WBN has been our prayer for sight. Eph.1:17,18 has been our continuous prayer before the Lord for the spirit of wisdom and revelation in the knowledge of Christ that the eyes of our understanding might be opened. God has been faithful to honor this posture before Him. What we have found is that spiritual understanding facilitates correct earthly action and decision making. It brings us into effective alignment with the Lord as He moves His purposes forward. Sight and understanding are the basis of partnership with the Lord. With them, we can effectively follow Him and act appropriately in the context of His plans. The desire for understanding should be the foundation prayer of every believer.

Participation Replaces Observation

Of course with understanding comes responsibility. One cannot pray for sight and understanding without the readiness to act based on what is revealed. Observation is the posture of the ignorant, who must look on without recognizing the significance of the events taking place before their eyes. Informed

> *Observation is the posture of the ignorant; informed action is the responsibility of those who have been given knowledge.*

action is the responsibility of those who have been given knowledge.

The final plague was the first one where it was not just Moses confronting Pharaoh. Throughout all the previous plagues Israel just stood by and observed what was going on. This position was due largely because they were ignorant of what was taking place around them. God spoke to Moses alone and therefore only Moses was empowered to act relevantly. Israel was not involved or responsible for any of the outcomes or decisions made in the progression of the clash between Moses and Pharaoh.

Now at the final plague participation replaces observation. The whole nation suddenly finds itself being required to participate in the unfolding of God's purposes in the crisis. And the basis of their participation was God speaking to them directly through the leadership of Moses. God's command to Moses in Exodus 12:3 was *"Speak to all the congregation of Israel."* Knowledge and understanding were now being delivered to them and when this happened, a critical shift occurred. The confrontation with Egypt was now no longer a responsibility for leaders alone to carry. Now all of God's people had to play their part. It was now no longer one man confronting Pharaoh, but an entire nation mobilizing against an empire.

Clear instructions are given to all of Israel. Every man and his household had to now mobilize for themselves in order to prepare for departure. Moses could declare the word of the Lord, but he himself could not personally activate its power as he did with the other plagues. The power of the word of the Lord at the point of exit is only activated through informed corporate participation. Passivity and mere observation had to be discarded and diligence, thoroughness and effort now had to come into effect. The final movement to liberation was a mass movement of the entire nation from passivity and inaccurate dependence upon leadership to informed action and personal responsibility that each man had to shoulder. Every man in Israel was made the partner of God.

Confidence Replaces Uncertainty

Then the children of Israel went away and did so; just as the LORD had commanded Moses and Aaron, so they did.

Exodus 12:28 (NKJV)

At the height of the confrontation, confidence replaces uncertainty. The verse here describes a picture of complete confidence in the direction of leadership. No longer do we have questions arising over Moses' right to command them. A powerful track record of nine devastating plagues had demolished any lack of certainty in the direction in which Moses was leading them. In the natural, the instructions and requirements for them would have seemed foolish. But they were coming from a man who had consistently walked before them in perfect partnership with the Lord. And the Lord Himself had consistently backed up His word through Moses before the eyes of the people. On that night, as the Lord walked through the land, there was a 0% mortality rate in the Israelite camp. Every house bore the mark of complete confidence in the word of the Lord delivered through spiritual leadership that had been certified through a long track record of partnership with God.

It is important to note here that the confidence which replaces uncertainty is not self-generated. Rather it comes from the surrounding context we find ourselves in. In other words, if there were no Moses leadership, no successful nine plagues, no track record of clear and accurate declaration of the mind of the Lord, no nation of people of similar conviction, there would have been no confidence to go forward. Accurate context brings confidence.

This is why it is so critical as we walk through the environment of the last days that believers concern themselves with the nature of the spiritual context in which they stand. For it is our spiritual context that will either deliver to us confidence to move forward or fear and uncertainty that paralyses.

Divine Direction Replaces Political Solutions

Then the officers of the children of Israel came and cried out to Pharaoh, saying, "Why are you dealing thus with your servants?

There is no straw given to your servants, and they say to us, 'Make brick!' And indeed your servants are beaten, but the fault is in your own people."

But he said, "You are idle! Idle! Therefore you say, 'Let us go and sacrifice to the LORD.'

Therefore go now and work; for no straw shall be given you, yet you shall deliver the quota of bricks.

And the officers of the children of Israel saw that they were in trouble** after it was said, "You shall not reduce any bricks from your daily quota."* ***Then, as they came out from Pharaoh, they met Moses and Aaron who stood there to meet them.

Exodus 5:15-19 (NKJV)

When the crisis began, the leaders of Israel opted for a political solution. This was their default stance. They believed that if they could negotiate politically and change things in the government, the issues could be resolved. They tried to reason with Pharaoh, but to no avail. The system was set on its course and no political action would resolve the problem. God had shut down all natural means of resolving the situation for Israel. They were left with only one option which was to look to God for a way out. Divine direction replaces political solutions.

There are no political solutions to the crises assaulting our societies on every level. Attempts to reason, collaborate and innovate are being frustrated at every turn. And once again the Lord is frustrating all other options for solutions except His direction. When the children of Israel came out from Pharaoh, Moses and Aaron *"stood there to meet them"* (Ex 5:19). They were being moved by God away from debating over government programs and towards the spiritual agenda which was the real cause of the conflict. It was a difficult shift for the people to make. At first Israel blamed these leaders for their misfortune and rejected their leadership. But as the crisis escalated, it became clear to all that Moses and Aaron were their only option. This is the beginning of the shift to partnership. It is the recognition that there are no solutions outside of Him. This is where the Israelites had to get to before the final plague could be initiated by God to grant them their freedom.

Faith Replaces Fear

On the night of the Passover, what brought terror and dread to Egypt brought salvation and liberation to Israel. Faith in God's promise replaced fear of reprisals by Egypt. And at the height of the crisis, a people lived their lives in faith for their future in God while others lived in fear of what tomorrow would bring. It is a distinction that God is prepared to make once again in our time. As we walk through the crisis of our time, within the nation of God Heaven must see a rising faith for the purposes of the Lord amidst the fear and uncertainty gripping the nations of the Earth.

God's purposes make a difference between the destruction taking place in the structures of Ancient Egypt and His preservation of the people of God. The Bible says that *"There shall be a great cry throughout all the land of Egypt, such as was not like it before, nor shall be like it again. But against none of the children of Israel shall a dog move its tongue, against man or beast, that you may know that the LORD does make a difference between the Egyptians and Israel"* (Ex 4:5-7). While crisis and meltdown terrorize the nations, not even a dog will bark against us. God wants us to know that He makes a distinction and He will keep us and watch over us in the crisis. The great cry that is echoing across Ancient Egypt will not reach us - not even a dog will bark against us or our house.

God is transforming His people just as He changed the Israelites thousands of years ago.

> *"And it came to pass at the end of the four hundred and thirty years — on that very same day — it came to pass that all **the armies of the LORD** went out from the land of Egypt."*
> *Exodus 12:41 (NKJV)*

The people were delivered from their slavery and they were made into the army of the Lord. With faith for God's promises filling their hearts, a nation of slaves were now recognized as the armies of the Lord capable of executing His judgments and purposes in perfect partnership with the mind of the Lord. May we all be numbered among this glorious company that is destined to walk the Earth before the End comes!

Chapter 31
The Sovereign Lord Does Nothing, Unless

In this book we have covered a lot of ground. We began with a description of the word of the Lord that Modern America is like Ancient Egypt, explaining our terms and the Biblical reality of prophetic metaphors. We then applied the word to over 400 years of America's history and although the scope is epic and historic it makes sense as we looked at the four phases of the empire. We could see God blessing the nation during its ascent and each one who is reading this could probably fill in a hundred examples of how His blessing manifests in the nation beyond what is written here.

This word from God is a macro prophetic view of God's ultimate purposes. It zooms out and looks at many vital issues from a broad scope displayed in the graphic below:

We looked at the history of the nation and the events that were orchestrated by a Sovereign God to bring us to this point. We also examined the spiritual reality which lies behind the decline, going beyond the political and peering deeply into God's intent and redemptive purpose. Time was taken to examine both the hardening and confrontation to explain events not only in America, but beyond it to all the nations.

Finally we moved into the *Transformation Imperatives* and saw that God wants to resource us. He is calling us to change and He is ready to make us, a generation of slaves, into His mighty army. This takes us beyond summarizing and into the more fundamental question:

Why did God speak this word to us?

To answer that question we have to deal with an apparent contradiction in the Bible found in Amos:

> *Surely the Lord GOD does nothing, Unless He reveals His secret to His servants the prophets.*
> *Amos 3:7 (NKJV)*

This verse joins two apparently opposite or conflicting realities. The first emphasizes God's might, His power and His sovereignty. Amos uses the two names of God (*Jehovah Adonai*) to emphasize the reality of God as Creator, Lord and Sovereign. The implication here is that the Lord is self-ruling and self-sufficient, not requiring the partnership, will or input of another to accomplish His divine objectives. Then, in the same breath, Amos declared the shocking reality that this Sovereign God would do nothing unless He first talks with man.

The voice of God lifts us into partnership with God's Sovereignty. It joins us to His purpose and allows us to participate with Him as He executes His purposes in the Earth. If God is indeed all-powerful, then certainly He is not doing this out of any deficiency in Himself. It is a matter of divine preference. God prefers to execute His purposes in partnership with us. What an ennobling and elevating thing for a human being to muse upon. God wants me as His partner. And according to this scripture in Amos, this partnership is expressed in God's willingness to share information about His actions before He acts.

Why did God speak this word to us? He is after people. We can personalize it and say *God is after you.* He wants you to participate with Him in His End Time purposes. He arranged for this book to come into your hands so you can understand what He is doing and rise to a place of boldness, confidence and participation in His plan. Partnership with God must be the direction of our lives as believers who live at the end of Time. And if we agree that we are closer to the end than any other generation, then as the people of God we should be closer to functional partnership with God than any other people. If we are closer to the end than any other generation, then the readiness of the Holy Spirit to make us God's functional partner is greatest in our time than ever before. All we have to do is to extend ourselves in faith and towards the values and positions of our final maturity in Christ.

The Parakletos

It is impossible to change and be like Christ, or to effectively inquire of the Lord, without the power of the Holy Spirit. He is the One sent to help us and make us like Christ:

...Unless I go away, the Advocate will not come to you; but if I go, I will send him to you.

But when he, the Spirit of truth, comes, he will guide you into all truth. He will not speak on his own; he will speak only what he hears, and he will tell you what is yet to come.

He will glorify me because it is from me that he will receive what he will make known to you.
                                                    John 16:7,13,14

The word for counselor (some versions say helper, others comforter) is *parakletos*. It literally means to be called to one's side or one's aid. It was used in a court of justice to denote a legal assistant or a counsel for the defense, an advocate. The Holy Spirit does not do the work for us, but He does come alongside and help us in our choices and the process of growth and development we commit to. He is the One who points out to us areas we need to grow and change in. We have listed 7 Transformation Imperatives and you can go to the website to interact with questions that will help you in considering how to change. But without the power of the Holy Spirit bringing transformation in our lives, it is just human effort that will fail.

In Congress WBN we are big believers in the Holy Spirit. We ask Him for spiritual sight and illumination. We inquire of Him and ask that He come alongside and assist us in our inquiry, taking us beyond our mental capacity and into the things of the Spirit. We interact with Him in areas of our lives which He puts His finger on, commanding us to change and then coming near to empower us to implement what He commands.

Unless the Lord builds the house, those who build labor in vain (Ps 127:1). Unless the insight given to us by God is implemented into our lives by the power of the Holy Spirit, we can read a book like this and believe it with our minds, but in the end accomplish nothing. We have asked the Holy Spirit for help in writing it. It was He who spoke this word to us and we have labored over each page to accurately describe and apply what God is saying. And now it is in your hands. What will you do with the word of the Lord? How will you rise to walk in partnership with God?

Epilogue

If you are reading this, then hopefully you have read this book in its entirety and have been challenged by its call to action and responsibility. The core motivation behind this book is to bring illumination and understanding concerning God's purpose in the midst of our present global environment of escalating crisis and perplexity. We are fully aware that what we have said here in many instances, challenges some basic assumptions that are held about Modern America and its role in the unfolding purposes of the Lord, the role and responsibility of the Church, the movement towards the End and most critically, about God Himself.

We are also aware that in some instances, this book, while it would have provided some answers and solutions, would have also raised some further questions. This we see as a good and beneficial thing. We hope that these questions launch you into deeper inquiry into the mind of God, His purposes and our placement within those purposes. After all, it is the glory of God to conceal a matter and the glory of kings to search it out. Keep searching and you will find.

To leaders, pastors and ministers of the Church, we would like to indicate clearly our desire for this book to be received as an invitation to dialogue. It is our desire to open discussion about the issues raised in this book and the prophetic word that the Lord has given to us about Modern

America and the current unfolding events in the Earth. We consider the opportunity to interact, discuss and share an invaluable one in the process of understanding what the Lord is doing in the Earth today. We invite you to visit our website, read our blogs and additional material and post your own responses. We would be happy to respond to queries and we will be keeping track of the feedback as it comes in. Please go to *www.arcofempires.org/interact.*

To our brothers in Christ, we hope that this book has provided an empowering perspective on what is taking place around us in the world today and has brought significant sight, hope, confidence and stability as you face the inevitable future. It is God's desire that we walk in light and understanding of His movements. It is our God-given right as His people to know the Divine Plan! We trust that you have been challenged to take up a new posture with respect to God's unfolding purposes and have accepted in your heart the challenge to walk in committed partnership with God through the Crisis to the End of Time. Our desire in writing has been two-fold: a) to bring you into a new appreciation of God's purpose to raise up a mature Church for the End Times, and b) to convince you that you are ordained to be a part of that great company of believers.

To those who do not yet know the Lord, now is the time! We hope that this book has explained in clear spiritual terms that we are living in a time unlike any other in the history of the earth. We have never been this close to the Finish, and as a consequence, the intent of the Lord to finalize all things is greatest in our time. We hope that this book has issued a call to you to make a decision that changes the direction of your life and brings your life into alignment with the plan of God. Our prayer is that beyond the perspectives shared on the escalating crisis in the Earth, that you have seen the heart of a Sovereign, redemptive

God whose overriding desire is that all should live and none should perish.

God is undoubtedly in the Earth. His feet are upon the nations and the full weight of His presence is being brought to bear upon the structures of life here in Time. As we see the escalating crisis around us, let us all look beyond this Earth to our life in eternity and begin to live in its eternal values and standards while still here locked in Time.

To order books and CDs by
Scott Webster
Or to make ministry contact
Please write or call:

Scott Webster Ministries
1860 Sandy Plains Road, Suite 204-410
Marietta, GA 30066
(678) 800-1796

E-mail: admin@scottwebsterministries.org
Visit our websites:
www.scottwebsterministries.org
www.congresswbn.org